STUDY GUIDE FOR

THE CODES GUIDEBOOK FOR INTERIORS

Sixth Edition

Sharon K. Harmon

Katherine E. Kennon

CONTENTS

INTRODUCTION

This sixth edition Study Guide has been updated to complement the new edition of *The Codes Guidebook for Interiors*. It is designed as a study tool. It can be used in the classroom as homework or for test problems, in conjunction with studio design projects, by an individual as a self-study tool, and by designers when preparing for the NCIDQ, ARE, and other licensing exams.

The Study Guide has been divided into four sections. Each section has been organized to parallel the 10 chapters in the *Guidebook* so that you can read a chapter in the book and then answer the corresponding questions in the Study Guide. Section 1 lists the key terms found in each chapter, which give you a general awareness of the topics in each chapter of the *Guidebook*. This section also provides you with a starting point for studying, allowing you to define and study the terms as you wish.

Section 2 concentrates on short-answer questions. These include true/false, fill-in-the-blank, and multiple-choice questions. The answers to these questions can be found within the text of the corresponding chapter in the *Guidebook*. The questions have been developed specifically to test your retention of the material within each chapter and to review the basic concepts presented within the text. (*Note*: The notes found in the margins of the *Guidebook* were not used in developing these questions.)

Section 3 of the Study Guide consists of study problems. Although some of the study problems are very direct and require memorization, most of the problems have been developed so that you can apply what you have learned to realistic design problems. As with the many examples provided in the *Guidebook*, a variety of design scenarios are used. Some of them test your ability to use the various code tables in the *Guidebook*. Other problems may require a code calculation or specific knowledge of a standard.

Section 4 provides you with the answers to the short-answer questions in Section 2. This section is invaluable. In addition to giving you the answers, it also offers an explanation of each answer. The answers to the study problems in Section 3 can be found in Section 5. They provide you with a comprehensive, step-by-step explanation of how the answers were obtained, including how to read each code table and how each calculation was determined.

The last part of the Study Guide consists of two appendices. Appendix A provides you with the code tables you are asked to reference when doing the study problems. They have been reprinted from the *Guidebook* for your convenience. In Appendix B, you will find all the checklists presented in the *Guidebook*. They have been reprinted in standard size so they will be easier to use. Feel free to copy and use them in your design projects.

As you work through this Study Guide, you will gain confidence in your knowledge of codes, standards, and federal regulations, and you will learn how to apply the codes to actual interior projects.

SECTION 1

KEY TERMS
BY CHAPTER

☐ CHAPTER 1: About the Codes

Access Board (ATBCB or U.S. Access Board)

Accessible

ABA Standards (2004)

ADA Standards (or *2010 ADA Standards*)

ADA-ABA Accessibility Guidelines (2004)

Alternative materials, design, and methods

American National Standards Institute (ANSI)

American Society of Heating, Refrigeration, and Air-Conditioning Engineers (ASHRAE)

Americans with Disabilities Act (ADA)

Americans with Disabilities Act Accessibility Guidelines (ADAAG, or 1994 ADA Standards)

American National Standards Institute (ANSI)

ANS process (ANS consensus process)

Architectural and Transportation Barriers Compliance Board (ATBCB or U.S. Access Board)

Architectural Barriers Act (ABA)

ASHRAE/IESNA 90.1 and 90.2

ASHRAE/USGBC/IES 189.1

ASTM International (ASTM)

Certification

Code

Code of Federal Regulations (CFR)

Commercial facility

Common Code Format

Department of Energy (DOE)

Department of Housing and Urban Development (HUD)

Department of Justice (DOJ)

Department of Transportation (DOT)

Energy Policy Act (EPAct)

Fair Housing Accessibility Guidelines (FHAG)

Fair Housing Act (FHA)

Federal Register (FR)

Federal regulation

Fire Code (NFPA 1)

ICC A117.1

ICC Performance Code for Buildings and Facilities (ICCPC)

International Building Code (IBC)

International Code Council (ICC)

International Energy Conservation Code (IECC)

International Existing Building Code (IEBC)

International Fire Code (IFC)

International Green Construction Code (IGCC)

International Mechanical Code (IMC)

International Plumbing Code (IPC)

International Residential Code (IRC)

Legacy code

Life Safety Code (LSC)

Manual of Style

National Electrical Code (NEC)

National Fire Protection Association (NFPA)

National Green Building Standard (NGBS or ICC 700)

NFPA 5000 Building Construction and Safety Code (NFPA 5000)

NSF International (NSF)

Performance code (or criteria)

Prescriptive code

Public accommodation

Safe harbor

Standard

Sustainability

Sustainable Design

Underwriters Laboratories (UL)

Uniform Federal Accessibility Standards (UFAS)

Uniform Mechanical Code (UMC)
Uniform Plumbing Code (UPC)
U.S. Green Building Council (USGBC)

☐ CHAPTER 2: Occupancy Classifications and Loads

Accessory occupancy
Ambulatory Health Care
Ancillary space
Assembly occupancy
Building type (or use)
Business occupancy
Detentional/correctional occupancy
Dwelling unit
Educational occupancy
Factory occupancy
Fixed seating
Floor area
Fuel load
Gross square feet
Habitable room
Hazard
Hazardous occupancy
Health Care occupancy
Incidental use
Industrial occupancy
Institutional occupancy
Live/work unit
Living area or room
Load factor
Mercantile occupancy
Mixed multiple occupancy
Net square feet
Non-separated mixed occupancy
Occupancy classification
Occupancy subclassification
Occupant
Occupant load
Occupiable space (or room)
Primary space (or use)
Residential occupancy

Risk factor
Separated mixed occupancy
Separated multiple occupancy
Sleeping area or room
Storage occupancy
Subclassification
Transient lodging
Utility occupancy

☐ CHAPTER 3: Construction Types and Building Sizes

Atrium
Basement
Building area
Building element
Building height
Combustible
Construction type
Fire resistance rating
Fire resistive
Fire retardant
Fire wall
Floor area
Heavy timber
High-rise building
Limited combustible
Mezzanine
Noncombustible
Party wall
Protected
Story
Structural element
Unprotected

☐ CHAPTER 4: Means of Egress

Accessible means of egress
Aisle
Aisle accessway

Alcove
Area of refuge
Clearance
Common path of travel
Corridor
Dead-end corridor
Discharge corridor
Door
Egress court
Elevator
Emergency lighting
Escalator
Exit
Exit access
Exit discharge
Exit passageway
Exit sign
Exit stair
Exit width
Exterior exit door
Foyer
Freight elevator
Guard
Half-diagonal rule
Handrail
Horizontal exit
Horizontal run
Intervening room
Landing
Means of egress
Moving walk
Multi-story building
Natural path of travel
Nosing
Occupant load
Passageway
Public way
Ramp
Riser
Stair variable
Stairway
Story
Travel distance
Tread
Turning space (or circle)
Unobstructed path

Vertical rise
Vestibule

☐ CHAPTER 5: Fire and Smoke Resistant Assemblies

Active fire protection system
Automatic closing
Ceiling damper
Ceramic glazing
Compartmentation
Construction assembly
Corridor Damper system
Demising wall
Draftstop
Evacuation
Fire area
Fire barrier
Fireblock
Fire damper
Fire door assembly
Fire exit hardware
Fire partition
Fire protection rating
Fire-rated assembly
Fire rating
Fire resistance rating
Firestop
Fire wall
Fire window assembly
Floor/ceiling assembly
F-rating
Fuel load
Glass block
Horizontal assembly
Horizontal exit
Incidental use
Label
Laminated glass
L-rating
Membrane penetration
Occupancy separation
Opening protective

Panic hardware
Party wall
Passive fire protection system
Rated glazing
Roof/ceiling assembly
Safety glass
Self-closing
Smoke barrier
Smoke compartment
Smoke damper
Smoke partition
Smokestop
Smokestop door
Sound transmission
Tenant separation
Test ratings
Through-penetration
Through-penetration protective
Transparent wall unit
T-rating
Vertical shaft enclosure
Vestibule
Wall assembly
Window assembly
Wired glass

❏ CHAPTER 6: Fire Protection Systems

Accessible warning system
Alarm system
Audible alarm
Automatic sprinkler system
Carbon monoxide detector
Deluge (sprinkler) system
Detection system
Dry pipe (sprinkler) system
Emergency communication system (ECS)
Extended coverage sprinkler head
Extinguishing system
Fast-response sprinkler head
Fire area

Fire detector
Fire extinguisher
Fire hose
Fire protection system
Fire zone
Heat detector
Initiating device
Integrated alarm
Large-drop sprinkler head
Manual fire alarm
Mass notification system (MNS)
Multiple-station detector
Open sprinkler head
Preaction (sprinkler) system
Quick-response sprinkler head
Residential sprinkler head
Single-station detector
Smoke detector
Sprinkler head
Standard spray head
Standpipe
Visual alarm
Wet pipe (sprinkler) system

❏ CHAPTER 7: Plumbing and Mechanical Requirements

Accessible fixture
Accessory
Ambulatory-accessible stall
Bathing room (or facility)
Bathroom
Bathtub
Clearance
Clear floor space
Clothes washer
Conditioned air
Cooling load
Damper
Demand control ventilation
Dishwasher
Drinking fountain

Duct system

Employee toilet facility

Energy efficiency

Exhaust

Family/Assisted-use facility

Front (or forward) approach

Grab bar

Hi-low drinking fountain

International Mechanical Code (IMC)

International Plumbing Code (IPC)

Kneespace

Lavatory

Makeup air

Mechanical room

Multiple bathing facility

Multiple-toilet facility

Occupant load

Parallel (or side) approach

Plenum system

Plumbing fixture

Potty parity

Privacy panel

Private (toilet) facility

Public toilet facility

Reach range

Return air

Shower

Signage

Single-bathing facility

Single-toilet facility

Sink

Supply (water, air, diffuser)Thermostat

Toespace

Toilet room or facility

Toilet stall

Turning space (or circle)

Uniform Mechanical Code (UMC)

Uniform Plumbing Code (UPC)

Unisex facility

Urinal

Utility sink

Ventilation

Water closet

Water conservation

Water consumption

WaterSense

Wheelchair-accessible stall

Zone

❏ **CHAPTER 8:
Electrical and
Communication
Requirements**

Alarm system

Appliance

Arc fault circuit interrupter (AFCI)

Armored (or flex or BX) cable

Assistive listening system

Audiovisual (AV) system

Automatic lighting shutoff

Backbone cabling

Bandwidth

Branch panelboard

Building automation system (BAS)

Cable

Cable tray

Circuit

Circuit breaker

Circuit integrity (CI) cable

Circuit interrupter

Coaxial cable

Communication room

Communication system

Composite (or hybrid) cable

Computer system

Conductor

Conduit

Dedicated circuit

Dedicated outlet

Demark

Device

Dual (or bi-level or split) switching

Electrical box

Electrical panel

Emergency power system (EPS)

Energy-efficient

ENERGY STAR

Equipment

Fail safe
Fail secure
Fiber optic cable
Fixture outlet
Flat wire
Ground fault circuit interrupter (GFCI)
Grounding
Horizontal cabling
Illumination level
Information technology
International Energy Conservation Code (IECC)
Junction box
Labeled [fixture or device]
Light fixture
Lighting outlet
Lighting power density (LPD)
Low-voltage cabling
Metal-clad cable
National Electrical Code (NEC or *NPFA 70)*
Nonmetallic-sheathed cable
Outlet
Outlet box
Overcurrent protective device
Panelboard
Public telephone
Raceway
Receptacle outlet
Renewable energy
Romex
Satellite room
Security system
Self-sustainable
Service entrance
Standby power system
Structured (or integrated or universal) cabling
Switch
Switchboard
Switch box
Tamper-resistant outlet
Technical power system
Telecommunication room
Telecommunication system
Telephone
Television system

Twisted-pair cable
Uninterrupted power supply (UPS)
Voice communication system
Wattage allowance
Wireway
Wireless
Zone cabling (or distribution)

☐ CHAPTER 9: Finish and Furniture Selection

California Technical Bulletin 133 (CAL 133 or *TB 133)*
Ceiling finishes
Ceiling treatment
Certificate of Flame Resistance
Char length
Cigarette Ignition Test
Component
Critical radiant flux (CRF)
Decorative material
Decorative vegetation
Detectable warning
Expanded vinyl wallcovering
Fabric
Finish
Finish classification (class)
Fire retardant
Flame retardant
Flame resistant
Flame source
Flame spread index (FSI)
Flammability
Flashover
Floor covering
Floor finishes
Foam (or cellular) plastic
Full-scale test
Furnishing finish
Furniture
Furring strip
Ignition source

Indoor air quality (IAQ)
Indoor environmental quality (IEQ)
Interior finish
Large-scale test
Light-transmitting plastic
Low emission
Mattress Test
Mock-up
Movable partition
Nontested finish
Offgas
Pass/fail test
Pill Test
Pitts Test (or *LC-50 Test*)
Plastic
Pretested finish
Radiant heat
Radiant Panel Test
Ranked rating
Rated test
Rating
Room Corner Tests
Safety glass
Seating
Site-fabrication stretch system
Small-scale test
Smoke Density Test
Smoke development index (SDI)
Smolder Resistance Test
Static coefficient of friction (SCOF)
Steiner Tunnel Test
Testing agency
Thermoplastic
Thermosetting plastic
Toxicity Test
Treated
Treatment company
Trim
Upholstered seating
Upholstered Seating Test
Upholstery
Vertical Flame Test
Vertical treatment
Volatile organic compound (VOC)
Wallcovering

Wall base
Wall finishes
Wall hanging
Window treatment
Worksurface

❑ CHAPTER 10: Code Officials and the Code Process

Appeal
Approved
Authority having jurisdiction (AHJ)
Board of Appeals
Building information modeling (BIM)
Building inspector
Certificate of Completion
Certificate of Occupancy (C of O)
Certified Building Official (CBO)
Code (or building) department
Code expeditor
Code official
Code publication
Code research
Compliance
Computer modeling
Construction documents
Construction drawings
Documentation
Final inspection
Fire marshal
Floor plan(s)
Green building program
Green rating system
Health code
Inspection
Jurisdiction
Liability
Local agency
Operation and maintenance (O & M) manual
Ordinance
Performance code

Performance design

Performance documentation

Permit

Phased Certificate of Occupancy

Plan review

Plans examiner

Preliminary review

Prescriptive code

Record (as-built) drawing(s)

Special inspector

Specification(s)

Temporary Certificate of Occupancy

Use and Occupancy letter (U and O)

Variance

SECTION 2

SHORT-ANSWER QUESTIONS

❑ CHAPTER 1: About the Codes

1. Federal buildings, such as VA hospitals and military office buildings, are usually not subject to state and local building codes. **True/False**

2. Typically, no two code jurisdictions have exactly the same codes and standards requirements. **True/False**

3. Many states have developed a custom building code using the *International Building Code* as the model. **True/False**

4. The NFPA *National Electrical Code* is the most widely used electrical code. **True/False**

5. The ADA is an accessibility code for the design of public buildings. **True/False**

6. Standards have no legal standing on their own. **True/False**

7. Codes and standards set only minimum criteria; when designing a project, stricter requirements can be followed. **True/False**

8. If it is decided that performance codes will be used on a project, the entire project must be designed using performance codes. **True/False**

9. The *Life Safety Code* is organized by the *Common Code Format*. **True/False**

10. Code requirements for indoor air quality (IAQ) were first introduced by the sustainability codes and standards. **True/False**

11. Which energy standard is required by the Energy Policy Act?

12. The *Life Safety Code* is different from the *International Building Code* because it organizes most of its chapters by _____.

13. What is another name for the Architectural and Transportation Barriers Compliance Board?

14. Which state developed the first sustainability code?

15. Which standards organization is recognized worldwide for its logo (or mark), which is attached to all products it approves?

16. Which of the following groups of codes is published as a separate document by the International Code Council, but not by the NFPA?
    a. Residential code, energy code, and green construction code
    b. Fire code, performance code, and residential code
    c. Performance code, residential code, and existing building code
    d. Existing building code, electrical code, and performance code

17. Which of the following is *not* a typical part of using performance codes?
    a. Working with a code official should begin in the early stages of the project.
    b. An overall team approach should be taken, with the client as the team leader.
    c. Supporting documentation should be provided to support your unique design.
    d. A number of parameters or risk factors should be determined at the beginning of the project.

18. When should you use a fire code in conjunction with a building code on a project?
    a. When it is required by the jurisdiction
    b. When you are designing for an occupancy that is considered more hazardous
    c. When you are working on a building that requires an emergency planning system
    d. a and b

19. Which of the following groups are all regulated by the ADA?
    a. Public transportation, federal buildings, telecommunication services
    b. Telecommunication services, public transportation, commercial facilities
    c. Commercial facilities, single-family homes, public transportation
    d. Federal office buildings, telecommunication services, commercial facilities

20. Which of the following is *not* a federal regulation?
    a. Americans with Disabilities Act
    b. Energy Policy Act
    c. Fair Housing Act
    d. All of the above are federal regulations

21. Which standards organization approves the standards developed by others rather than concentrating on developing its own?
    a. ANSI
    b. UL
    c. ASHRAE
    d. ASTM

22. Which of the following publications does *not* address accessibility issues?
    a. UFAS
    b. ADA
    c. ICC A117.1
    d. All of the above address accessibility issues

23. What do you do if you are required to use two different code publications for a project and there is a conflict between the code requirements?
    a. Use the requirement found in the most recent code publication.
    b. Compare the two requirements and use the most restrictive one.
    c. Pick one or the other as long as it is required by one of the publications.
    d. None of the above.

24. Energy-related requirements that are enforced on a state and/or local level are most likely the result of which federal legislation?
    a. ADA
    b. EPAct
    c. FHA
    d. None of the above

25. Which of the following statements concerning sustainability codes is correct?
    a. The *IGCC* was developed by the ICC to coordinate with the other I-Codes.
    b. The *NGBS* was the first sustainability code to be developed.
    c. The *IECC* is considered a sustainability code.
    d. a and c

☐ CHAPTER 2: Occupancy Classifications and Loads

1. Determining the occupancy classification(s) of a project should be one of the first steps in researching codes. **True/False**

2. If there are two occupancies in the same building, the larger occupancy is considered the main occupancy and the smaller occupancy is known as the accessory occupancy. **True/False**

3. Subcategories of occupancy classifications such as Assembly and Institutional only affect the occupant load of a project. **True/False**

4. Locations of fire resistance-rated walls can affect how codes apply in buildings with more than one occupancy classification. **True/False**

5. If two different occupancies are separated by a nonrated wall, they can be considered a separated mixed occupancy. **True/False**

6. The number of occupants receiving care, not the total occupant load, determines if an assisted living facility is considered an Institutional occupancy or a Residential occupancy. **True/False**

7. The number of children receiving care determines whether a preschool is considered Institutional or Educational. **True/False**

8. The size of the space determines if an indoor pool is considered an A-3 or an A-4. **True/False**

9. When designing a restaurant in a jurisdiction that enforces the *International Building Code* and the *Life Safety Code,* which *three* occupancy classifications should be considered?
   _____ _____ _____

10. The occupancies that would be considered Institutional by the *International Building Code* are designated differently by the *Life Safety Code.* Name the *two* corresponding LSC occupancy classifications: _____ _____.

11. The various types of hazardous situations that can occur in a building are also often referred to as _____ by the codes.

12. When measuring a building to determine the occupant load, _____ square feet (square meters) refers to the building area that includes all miscellaneous (or ancillary) spaces.

13. The codes divide the type of hazardous occupancies into four main categories: fire, explosive, _____, and _____.

14. Using the *International Building Code* classifications, match each building type on the left with its typical occupancy classification shown on the right. Fill in the appropriate letter on the lines shown.

___ Supermarket	**a.** Institutional occupancy
___ Refinery	**b.** Hazardous occupancy
___ Gas plant	**c.** Business occupancy
___ Bank	**d.** Assembly occupancy
___ Nursing home	**e.** Storage occupancy
___ Kindergarten	**f.** Mercantile occupancy
___ Dormitory	**g.** Industrial occupancy
___ Church	**h.** Educational occupancy
___ Freight terminal	**i.** Residential occupancy

15. Which three items help to determine the occupancy classification or subclassification of a project?
    a. Type of hazards, type of activity occurring, size of building
    b. Size of the building, type of wall ratings, type of activity occurring
    c. Type of activity occurring, type of hazards, number of occupants
    d. Size of the building, number of occupants, type of wall ratings

16. The *Life Safety Code* distinguishes between new and existing occupancies. Which of the following scenarios would *not* create a new occupancy?
    a. A project that was designed but not occupied before the new edition of the code was enforced
    b. A company that is hiring a number of new employees
    c. A company that is relocating to another building
    d. A company that is moving into its new office headquarters

17. In the *International Building Code,* which of the following occupancies might be assigned to different subclassifications depending on the number of occupants?
    a. Assembly and Institutional
    b. Educational and Residential
    c. Assembly and Educational
    d. Residential and Institutional

18. Which of the following use types is usually *not* considered an Educational occupancy?
    a. College classrooms
    b. High school classrooms
    c. Elementary school classrooms
    d. Preschool classrooms

19. Which of the following building types may *not* always be considered a Residential occupancy?
    a. Monasteries
    b. Halfway houses
    c. Nursing homes
    d. Hotels

20. Which of the following building types would be the least likely to be a mixed occupancy?
    a. Restaurant
    b. High-security prison
    c. High school
    d. Hotel

21. Which of the following occupancy classifications is currently *not* heavily regulated as a public accommodation by the Americans with Disabilities Act?
    a. Institutional
    b. Business
    c. Factory
    d. Mercantile

22. Which of the following statements about accessory occupancies is *not* true?
    a. When an accessory occupancy exists within a primary occupancy, most of the code requirements are based on the primary occupancy.
    b. The area of an accessory occupancy must be less than 10 percent of the primary occupancy's area.
    c. To be considered an accessory occupancy, the allowable area within the construction type of a building or space must also be considered.
    d. All of the above items are true.

23. When there is more than one type of occupancy in the same building, in which case must they meet the requirements of the most stringent occupancy classification?
    a. If they are considered separated mixed occupancies
    b. If they are considered non-separated mixed occupancies
    c. If they are considered mixed multiple occupancies
    d. b and c

24. In some cases, you may decide to increase the occupant load of a space so that it is higher than that determined by the load factor. When you do so, you must also do which of the following?
    a. Make sure you provide additional exiting as required for the increased number.
    b. Make sure all the walls within the building or space are rated.
    c. Typically, get approval from a code official for the increased number.
    d. a and c

25. The occupant load is *not* needed to determine which of the following?
    a. The total required exit width for the space
    b. The maximum number of people allowed in the space
    c. The construction type of the building
    d. The number of plumbing fixtures required for the space

26. What do you need to know in order to determine the required occupant load for a space?
    a. Load factor and square footage
    b. Building type and occupancy classification
    c. Number of occupants and load factor
    d. Load factor and building type

27. When a building has a mixed occupancy, the occupant load for the whole building is determined by which of the following?
    a. The occupancy that allows the largest number of people
    b. The occupancy with the most square feet (square meters)
    c. The occupancy with the highest load factor
    d. The requirements of each occupancy combined together

28. If a space has multiple uses, the occupant load for that space is determined by which of the following?
    a. The use that indicates the largest concentration of people
    b. The use that occupies the space the most often
    c. The use that has the highest load factor
    d. The total occupant load for all the uses

29. When calculating occupant loads, which of the following determines if the seats are considered fixed?
   a. The seats are not easily moved.
   b. The seats are continuous, without arms.
   c. The seats are used on a more permanent basis.
   d. All of the above

30. Which of the following is *not* true about live/work units?
   a. The unit is considered a live/work unit as long as the nonresidential portion of the unit is greater than 10 percent of the space.
   b. The total area of the unit is not regulated by the code.
   c. A typical home office could be considered a live/work unit.
   d. All of the above are incorrect.

☐ CHAPTER 3: Construction Types and Building Sizes

1. Interior walls and partitions are required to be rated in Type I and Type II construction. **True/False**

2. When comparing the different types of construction, Type V is considered the least restrictive and requires the lowest fire ratings. **True/False**

3. Most combustible construction materials can be treated to gain some amount of fire resistance. **True/False**

4. Buildings must consistently be updated to meet the construction type requirements within the newest building codes. **True/False**

5. The distance of an adjacent building can affect the allowed size of a new building. **True/False**

6. A fire _____ construction material will not be affected by flame, heat, or hot gases.

7. Load-bearing walls, columns, and shaft enclosures are often considered _____ elements by the building codes.

8. Wood that is considered fire resistant because of its large diameter is called _____ _____.

9. Which of the following statements about construction types is *not* correct?
   a. The main difference between Type I and Type II is the required hourly ratings.
   b. Determining if an existing building is a Type I or Type II can be difficult because they often require the same types of construction materials.
   c. Combustible materials are not allowed in Type I but they are allowed in Type II.
   d. All of the above are correct.

10. Which construction type consists of exterior walls that are noncombustible but allows interior elements to consist of combustible materials?
    a. Type II
    b. Type III
    c. Type IV
    d. Type V

11. Which of the following statements about building materials is *not* correct?
    a. Unless encased in a protective coating, iron and steel will have a rapid loss of strength should a fire occur.
    b. Chemically treated wood is often known as flame resistant–treated wood.
    c. Noncombustible materials typically consist of brick, concrete, and steel.
    d. All of the above are correct.

12. Which of the following statements about fire-retardant materials is *not* correct?
    a. They will not contribute to the fuel of the fire.
    b. They will delay the spread of a fire for a designated time period.
    c. They can sometimes be substituted for materials required to be noncombustible.
    d. All of the above are correct.

13. If more than one type of construction exists within a single building, each type of construction must be separated from the other by which of the following?
    a. Parapet wall or party wall
    b. Party wall or occupant separation wall
    c. Fire wall or party wall
    d. Occupancy separation wall or fire wall

14. Which of the following occupancy classifications typically require the strictest types of construction?
    a. Assembly and Institutional occupancies
    b. Assembly and Residential occupancies
    c. Mercantile and Assembly occupancies
    d. Institutional and Residential occupancies

15. To determine if a certain occupancy classification can be located in a specific building, which of the following do you need to know?
    a. The construction type of the building
    b. The square footage (square meters) or area of the building
    c. If the building is sprinklered
    d. All of the above

16. Which of the following limits a building's maximum size?
    a. Construction type(s)
    b. Occupancy classification(s)
    c. Proximity to other buildings
    d. All of the above

17. Which of the following would be allowed by the codes as a way of increasing the allowable area of a building?
    a. Changing the construction type from Type III to Type IV
    b. Adding more occupancy separation walls
    c. Adding an automatic sprinkler system
    d. a and c

18. Which of the following would *not* affect the construction type during an interior renovation?
    a. Adding an opening in a structural wall
    b. Installing a ceramic tile floor over concrete
    c. Changing the ceiling tiles in a rated suspended ceiling
    d. Recessing a shower unit in a concrete slab

19. Which of the following would contribute to the sustainability of a building?
    a. Use of a steel structure
    b. Management of the product waste during construction
    c. Use of a local concrete supplier
    d. All of the above

☐ CHAPTER 4: Means of Egress

1. Every path of travel throughout a building can be considered a means of egress. **True/False**

2. All interior egress doors must swing in the direction of travel to the exit. **True/False**

3. If the width of an alley or sidewalk is more than 10 feet (3048 mm) wide, it is no longer considered a public way. **True/False**

4. The main difference between a corridor and an aisle is that a corridor is typically surrounded by full-height walls and an aisle is created by furniture or equipment. **True/False**

5. No doorway can be more than 48 inches (1220 mm) wide. **True/False**

6. When determining the number of exits in a multi-story building, the floor with the largest occupant load determines the number of required exits for all lower floors that lead to the ground level. **True/False**

7. Name the *three* main interior-related components of a means of egress. _____

8. What component of a means of egress is sometimes required for persons with disabilities? _____

9. The final destination in a means of egress is always a _____.

10. What are *two* types of door pulls that can be considered accessible?

11. A stairway must have an intermediate landing if it rises more than how many feet or millimeters? _____ _____

12. In addition to an exit sign, name another type of exiting sign that may be required by the codes: _____

13. A fire resistance–rated corridor that connects the bottom of an exit stair to an exterior exit door is called an exit _____.

14. When three exits are required in a space, the third exit should be placed as _____ as possible.

15. Name the *two* types of means of egress illumination required by the code in a high-rise building. _____ _____

16. Match the scenarios on the left with the means of egress components shown on the right. Fill in the appropriate letter on the lines shown. (Note that letters may be used more than once.)

   ___ An exterior door   **a.** Exit access
   ___ A corridor   **b.** Exit
   ___ An office   **c.** Exit discharge
   ___ A stairwell   **d.** Public way
   ___ After descending four flights of stairs, you leave the stairwell and find yourself in the lobby
   ___ An alley that is 8 feet (2438 mm) wide but open to the sky
   ___ An aisle in an open office area between furniture system workstations

17. Which of the following are affected by means of egress requirements?
   a. Finish selections
   b. Occupant loads
   c. Fire ratings of walls
   d. a and c

18. Which of the following statements about a means of egress is *not* correct?
   a. It is a continuous and unobstructed path of travel.
   b. It can consist of vertical and horizontal passageways.
   c. It affects all buildings, new and existing.
   d. All of the above are correct.

19. Foyers and vestibules are examples of which of the following?
   a. Exit discharges
   b. Public ways
   c. Exit accesses
   d. Exits

20. Which of the following means of egress must always be fully enclosed?
   a. Intervening room
   b. Exit stair
   c. Exit access stairs
   d. All of the above

21. What is the typical head clearance required in an exit and exit access way?
   a. 80 inches (2030 mm)
   b. 84 inches (2134 mm)
   c. 90 inches (2286 mm)
   d. 96 inches (2440 mm)

22. Which of the following is *not* considered a type of exit?
   a. Exit stair
   b. Exit corridor
   c. Exterior door
   d. Horizontal exit

23. An accessible ramp in a means of egress should have a slope no greater than what ratio?
    a. 1:8
    b. 1:12
    c. 1:18
    d. 1:20

24. Which of the following statements about interior means of egress doors is *not* correct?
    a. They must have a minimum clear opening that is 36 inches (914 mm) wide.
    b. The floor level on both sides of the door cannot be more than $\frac{1}{2}$ inch (13 mm) below the top of the threshold.
    c. They cannot reduce any required landing by more than 7 inches (178 mm) when fully open.
    d. All of the above are correct.

25. Which of the following statements about stair-related codes is correct?
    a. The minimum riser height is 7 inches (178 mm).
    b. The minimum tread length is 11 inches (279 mm).
    c. Spiral stairs are not allowed in the means of egress.
    d. Handrails are always required on both sides of the stairs.

26. Horizontal exits are most commonly found in which of the following occupancy classifications?
    a. Institutional occupancies
    b. Mercantile occupancies
    c. Residential occupancies
    d. Educational occupancies

27. Which of the following would most likely *not* be allowed as an intervening room as required by the means of egress codes?
    a. A reception area in an accounting firm
    b. A secretarial area in a law firm
    c. A file/supply room in an advertising firm
    d. A front lobby in a large brokerage firm

28. If an elevator is used as an exit in a means of egress, which of the following statements would *not* be correct?
    a. The elevator is required to have an area of refuge located somewhere in each floor.
    b. The elevator shaft and the adjacent lobby on each floor are required to be fire rated.
    c. The elevator is required to be connected to standby power.
    d. All of the above are correct.

29. Which of the following items are typically required at an area of refuge?
    a. A two-way communication device
    b. A sprinkler system
    c. A clear floor space
    d. a and c

30. Which of the following statements is *not* correct?
    a. To calculate the exit widths for a whole building, you must calculate the occupant load for each floor separately.
    b. To calculate the exit widths for a whole floor with different occupancies, you must calculate the occupant load based on the tenant with the highest load factor.
    c. To calculate the exit widths for a corridor connecting several tenants, you must calculate the total occupant load for the floor.
    d. All of the above are correct.

31. What is the typical minimum corridor width required by the building codes in most occupancies?
    a. 32 inches (8135 mm)
    b. 36 inches (914 mm)
    c. 44 inches (1118 mm)
    d. 48 inches (1219 mm)

32. In most cases, nothing is allowed to reduce the width of an exit. Which of the following is a typical exception allowed by the codes?
    a. Doors that do not project more than 7 inches (178 mm) when fully open
    b. Wall trim that is less than $\frac{1}{2}$ inch (13 mm) thick
    c. Handrails that meet ADA requirements
    d. All of the above

33. What is the term for the maximum distance a person should have to travel from any position in a building to the nearest exit?
    a. Means of egress
    b. Natural path of travel
    c. Common path of travel
    d. Travel distance

34. What is the maximum dead-end corridor length typically allowed by the codes in a nonsprinklered building?
    a. 15 feet (4572 mm)
    b. 20 feet (6096 mm)
    c. 25 feet (7620 mm)
    d. 30 feet (9144 mm)

35. Correctly calculating the occupant load of a space is important for determining which of the following?
    a. The number of exits
    b. The width of an exit
    c. The location of an exit
    d. a and b

36. Which of the following statements is *not* correct?
    a. The width of an exit access corridor can typically be based on half of the required occupant load if it leads to two separate exits on the same floor.
    b. The width of an exit stairway can sometimes be reduced as it travels toward the exit discharge.
    c. One exit is often allowed in small buildings or spaces, depending on the number of occupants and/or the travel distance.
    d. All of the above are correct.

37. Which of the following statements about aisle access ways at tables and chairs is *not* correct?
    a. Their required width is measured to the back of the chair, not the table.
    b. Their required width is usually less than that of the adjacent aisle.
    c. 18 inches (457 mm) is the width assumed by the code to be needed for a chair.
    d. Their required width may have to be increased in some cases to allow for accessibility.

38. Which of the following codes can affect the requirements of a stair?
    a. *IBC*
    b. *LSC*
    c. *ICCPC*
    d. All of the above

CHAPTER 5: Fire and Smoke Resistant Assemblies

1. An active fire protection system sometimes is referred to as a prevention system. **True/False**

2. The fire resistance rating of a floor/ceiling assembly is controlled only by the construction type of the building. **True/False**

3. All fire protection rated doors must have an automatic closing device. **True/False**

4. The fire rating of a through-penetration is typically lower than the fire rating of the construction assembly it is penetrating. **True/False**

5. A fire-rated door can also be used as a smokestop door. **True/False**

6. If compartmentation is required, fire barriers are used to create the compartmentation. **True/False**

7. Occupancy separation walls and demising walls are the same thing. **True/False**

8. Doors with fire protection ratings are not allowed to have glass lites as part of the door. **True/False**

9. Walls that are used to create a vertical separation within a building or between two different buildings are called _____ walls.

10. A door assembly consists of a door, frame, and _____.

11. Which restricts the passage of smoke, a smoke barrier or a smoke partition? _____

12. Match each *NFPA* standard on the left with the number designation shown on the right. Fill in the appropriate letter on the lines shown.
    __ *Installation of Smoke Door Assemblies and Other Opening Protectives*   **a.** *NFPA 105*
    __ *Fire Doors and Other Opening Protectives*   **b.** *NFPA 252*
    __ *Fire Test for Window and Glass Block Assemblies*   **c.** *NFPA 221*
    __ *Fire Tests of Door Assemblies*   **d.** *NFPA 251*
    __ *Test of Fire Resistance of Building Construction and Materials*   **e.** *NFPA 80*
    __ *High-Challenge Fire Walls, Fire Walls, and Fire Barrier Walls*   **f.** *NFPA 257*

13. What is the typical fire resistance rating of an exit access corridor in a nonsprinklered building?
    a. 2 hour
    b. $1\frac{1}{2}$ hour
    c. 1 hour
    d. No rating is required.

14. Which of the following statements about firestops is correct?
    a. They are required at through-penetrations in fire barriers.
    b. They are a means of restricting the passage of heat and flames, but not necessarily smoke, in concealed spaces.
    c. A firestop device must be used to create the firestop.
    d. a and b

15. A wall assembly with a 2-hour fire resistance rating is typically required for which means of egress?
   a. Exit access
   b. Public way
   c. Exit discharge
   d. Exit

16. Which of the following devices is used to prevent the movement of air, smoke, gases, and flame through large concealed spaces?
   a. Firestops
   b. Draftstops
   c. Fireblocking
   d. Dampers

17. Which of the following is *not* a characteristic of a "labeled" window?
   a. It is a fire protection–rated window.
   b. It has a label that is permanently attached.
   c. It is required to be tempered.
   d. It has been tested by a nationally recognized testing company.

18. Which of the following statements about occupancy separation is *not* correct?
   a. It is required in a mixed-occupancy building, but not necessarily in a multiple-occupancy building.
   b. When two different occupancies are adjacent to each other, the one requiring the higher rating applies.
   c. It may be required within a single tenant space if the space includes more than one occupancy.
   d. It includes vertical separation and horizontal separation.

19. Which of the following types of glass is typically considered to have a fire protection rating?
   a. Laminated glass
   b. Tempered glass
   c. Glass block
   d. a and c

20. Which of the following smoke compartments require special ventilation and air circulation?
   a. Stair shafts
   b. Linen chutes
   c. Vestibules
   d. All of the above

21. Which of the following statements about fire-rated doors is correct?
   a. A variety of rated glazing materials can be used as lites in fire-rated doors.
   b. All fire-rated doors must undergo the hose stream test.
   c. Only certain fire-rated doors must be labeled.
   d. Fire-rated doors cannot include glazing components.

22. Which of the following is typically considered a fire partition by the *International Building Code*?
   a. A wall between two guest rooms in a hotel
   b. A wall between an office space and an exit access corridor
   c. A wall between two tenants in a shopping mall
   d. a and c

23. Which of the following fire tests is required for safety glazing?
    a. *ASTM E152*
    b. *NFPA 252*
    c. *ANSI Z97.1*
    d. *UL 10B*

24. Which of the following can be used to help control smoke during a fire?
    a. Smoke barriers
    b. Pressurized exits
    c. Sprinklers
    d. a and b

25. Which type of through-penetration is required in a duct that extends through a rated floor assembly?
    a. Draftstop
    b. Fire damper
    c. Ceiling damper
    d. None of the above

26. Which of the following statements about smoke dampers is *not* correct?
    a. Smoke dampers are typically used in ducts that penetrate smoke barriers.
    b. Smoke dampers are usually installed with a smoke detector.
    c. Smoke dampers are typically installed adjacent to a duct.
    d. All of the above are correct.

27. Which of the following would compromise the rating of a 1-hour fire resistant wall assembly?
    a. Using a building material differently than specified by the manufacturer
    b. Not using rated caulk at the seams and joints
    c. Installing an electrical box in the wall cavity for a switch
    d. a and b

28. If rated glazing is required in a location where human impact is a concern, which glazing product would meet both fire protection and impact resistance requirements?
    a. Clear ceramic
    b. Wired glass
    c. Laminated glass
    d. a and c

29. Which is *not* a method to determine if a wall is rated?
    a. Check with the maintenance department
    b. Check to see if the wall is labeled above the ceiling
    c. Check the original construction documents
    d. Check to see if the door has a label

CHAPTER 6: Fire Protection Systems

1. Only multiple-station smoke detectors are required by the codes to be tied into the building's power source, but single-station smoke detectors are not.   **True/False**

2. The decision to use an automatic sprinkler system, fire detection system, or smoke detection system is mostly based on budgetary concerns.   **True/False**

3. The codes do not allow the connection of fire and smoke alarm systems to the building's security system.   **True/False**

4. When a fire occurs, a detection system only detects the presence of smoke.   **True/False**

5. An alarm can be activated both manually and automatically.   **True/False**

6. Manual fire alarms must typically be placed within 5 feet (1524 mm) from the latch side of an exit door.   **True/False**

7. Fire extinguishers must be in a glass case mounted on the wall.   **True/False**

8. Most alarms must be audible and _____.

9. When required in a Class A space, the codes typically require that no occupant can be more than how many feet or millimeters from a fire extinguisher?

10. Match each *NFPA* standard on the left with the number designation shown on the right. Fill in the appropriate letter on the lines shown.
    __ *Portable Fire Extinguishers*   **a.**   *NFPA 70*
    __ *National Fire Alarm Code and Signaling Code*   **b.**   *NFPA 110*
    __ *National Electrical Code*   **c.**   *NFPA 12*
    __ *Installation of Sprinkler Systems*   **d.**   *NFPA 10*
    __ *Emergency and Standby Power Systems*   **e.**   *NFPA 72*
    __ *Fire Safety and Emergency Symbols*   **f.**   *NFPA 13*
    __ *Carbon Dioxide Extinguishing Systems*   **g.**   *NFPA 170*

11. What type of system directs occupants out of the building during an emergency by verbal command?
    a.   Emergency voice alarm communication system
    b.   Accessible warning system
    c.   Visual/audible alarm system
    d.   a and c

12. When specifying a visual alarm, which of the following are regulated by the codes and the *ADA Standards*?
    a.   Height
    b.   Color and intensity
    c.   Flash rate and duration
    d.   All of the above

13. Which of the following is *not* considered a detection system?
    a. Smoke or heat detectors
    b. Manual fire alarms
    c. Firestops
    d. b and c

14. Which of the following statements about detection systems is correct?
    a. Smoke detectors should be located next to the intersection of a wall or ceiling.
    b. If heat detectors are used, smoke detectors are not necessary for accurate detection.
    c. Smoke detectors are especially effective in detecting smoldering fires.
    d. All of the above are correct.

15. Which of the following is *not* considered an alarm system?
    a. Accessible warning system
    b. Manual fire alarm
    c. Voice communication system
    d. Mass notification system

16. Which of the following statements about an EVACS is *not* correct?
    a. It provides direction to the occupants during an emergency.
    b. Its speaker locations are based on paging zones created within the building.
    c. It is required in most occupancy classifications.
    d. It is similar to a public address system.

17. Which class of standpipe is designed for use by building occupants?
    a. Class I
    b. Class II
    c. Class III
    d. b and c

18. Which of the following is *not* typically used by the codes to determine if a standpipe is required in a building?
    a. The number of stories in the building
    b. The number of stairwells in the building
    c. A sprinkler system is located in the building
    d. The type of occupancy located in the building

19. Which of the following would affect the need for a sprinkler system?
    a. Building size
    b. Occupancy type
    c. Specific room use
    d. All of the above

20. Which type of sprinkler system would typically be used where the system would be exposed to freezing temperatures?
    a. Wet pipe system
    b. Dry pipe system
    c. Deluge system
    d. Fast-response system

21. Which of the following is *not* typically allowed by the codes because a sprinkler system is provided?
    a. A reclassified occupancy type
    b. An increased travel distance
    c. A lower finish classification
    d. A lower fire resistance rating of a structural element

22. Which of the following is *not* a type of sprinkler head?
    a. Residential
    b. Pendant
    c. Large-drop
    d. Fast-response

23. How much clearance is typically required below the head or deflector of a sprinkler?
    a. 12 inches (305 mm)
    b. 18 inches (457 mm)
    c. 24 inches (610 mm)
    d. 30 inches (762 mm)

24. Which of the following statements about fire-related codes is *not* correct?
    a. They control building materials such as ducts, wiring, and pipes.
    b. They are affected by accessibility codes.
    c. They include provisions for fire protection and smoke protection.
    d. All of the above are correct.

25. Which of the following specialty types of rooms or areas is the most likely to use a non-water-based fire extinguishing system?
    a. Restaurant kitchen
    b. Atrium
    c. Trash chute
    d. Boiler room

26. Which of the following sprinkler head orientations are available recessed and surface mounted?
    a. Pendant and sidewall
    b. Upright and pendant
    c. Concealed and sidewall
    d. Upright and concealed

CHAPTER 7: Plumbing and Mechanical Requirements

1. Plumbing requirements are found in the building code and the plumbing code.   **True/False**

2. The general rule for plumbing fixtures is that every floor in a building will require at least two toilet facilities.   **True/False**

3. In larger restrooms, there are usually more lavatories than water closets.   **True/False**

4. Coordination between plumbing and mechanical has more impact on a project than coordination of plumbing and electrical systems.   **True/False**

5. Water consumption requirements for plumbing fixtures are found in the plumbing codes and the energy codes.   **True/False**

6. The mechanical codes are the only resource for mechanical requirements.   **True/False**

7. A mechanical room is not typically required to meet accessibility requirements.   **True/False**

8. On smaller plumbing projects where an engineer is not required by the codes or local jurisdiction, a licensed _____ can do the work directly from your drawings.

9. All plumbing fixtures must have a smooth, _____ finish.

10. If a urinal is used in a project, it is usually substituted for a required

    _____.

11. What is the maximum depth of an accessible kitchen or break room sink in inches or millimeters? _____

12. HVAC stands for heating, _____, and air-conditioning.

13. The cooling _____ refers to how much energy is required to cool a space.

14. Which of the following is tied to the plumbing system of a building and may involve the services of a plumbing engineer if required on a project?
    a. Standpipes and fire hoses
    b. Sprinklers and drinking fountains
    c. Water closets and lavatories
    d. All of the above

15. What is the first item you need to determine when you are planning the layout of a toilet facility?
    a. The occupancy classification
    b. The type of fixtures required
    c. The number of fixtures required
    d. The actual number of occupants

16. Which of the following statements about calculating the number of plumbing fixtures is *not* correct?
    a. The total occupant load for a space should be divided in half before using the ratios in the plumbing fixture table to determine the number of plumbing fixtures.
    b. If you are calculating the number of plumbing fixtures for multiple occupancies on the same floor, any fractional numbers should be rounded up before adding them together to obtain the total number of fixtures.
    c. When dividing the total occupant load in half results in a fraction, this fraction should be used; only the final number of plumbing fixtures should be rounded up when necessary.
    d. a and c

17. Which of the following statements about plumbing fixtures is *not* correct?
    a. The number of urinals allowed in a male restroom is based on the quantity of water closets.
    b. Travel distance can limit the number of fixtures that can be grouped together.
    c. If a tenant space has its own toilet facility, it can be deducted from the total facilities required for that floor.
    d. All of the above are correct.

18. Which of the following statements about accessible toilet facilities is *not* correct?
    a. A single accessible toilet facility may be allowed in some existing buildings.
    b. Separate toilet facilities do not have to be provided for employees and customers.
    c. When a building has multiple toilet facilities, a percentage of them must be accessible.
    d. When a single urinal is required in a toilet facility, it must be accessible.

19. Which of the following statements about required unisex facilities is correct?
    a. Unisex toilet facilities are also referred to as family/assisted-use facilities.
    b. A unisex toilet facility is usually required if more than eight water closets are provided.
    c. If a required unisex facility is included, it is not counted in the total number of plumbing fixtures.
    d. None of the above are correct.

20. Which of the following plumbing requirements is *not* controlled by the ADA guidelines and standards?
    a. Ease of controls
    b. Minimum clearances
    c. Reach ranges
    d. Fixture finishes

21. What is the typical accessible distance required between the centerline of a water closet and the side wall?
    A. 24 inches (610 mm)
    B. 18 inches (455 mm)
    C. 15 inches (381 mm)
    D. 10 inches (254 mm)

22. Urinals are most commonly used in which occupancy classifications?
    a. Assembly and Educational occupancies
    b. Assembly and Mercantile occupancies
    c. Mercantile and Institutional occupancies
    d. Educational and Institutional occupancies

23. Which of the following statements about drinking fountains is *not* correct?
    a. Two drinking fountains are required on each floor of a building, one at standing height and one at wheelchair height.
    b. A clear floor space 30 by 48 inches (760 by 1220 mm) is required at all accessible drinking fountains.
    c. The front edge of a drinking fountain cannot protrude more than 4 inches (100 mm) into a path of accessible travel
    d. All of the above are correct.

24. What is the minimum diameter of the turning circle required in all accessible toilet facilities?
    a. 48 inches (1220 mm)
    b. 60 inches (1525 mm)
    c. 66 inches (1675 mm)
    d. 72 inches (1830 mm)

25. Which of the following statements is correct?
    a. Bathtubs are required by the codes in a wide variety of occupancies.
    b. The swing of the door to an accessible toilet stall does not affect the size of the stall.
    c. The codes control the shape of the seat on a water closet.
    d. Accessible sinks require more clear kneespace than lavatories.

26. If you were designing the layout of a multiple-toilet facility, which of the following would *not* meet codes?
    a. Adding a vestibule before you get to the restroom door
    b. Locating a drinking fountain in the vestibule leading to the restroom
    c. Using plastic-laminate toilet stalls
    d. Mounting all toilet accessories at accessible heights

27. What is the typical floor clearance required at most accessible plumbing fixtures and accessories?
    a. 36 by 40 inches (915 by 1015 mm)
    b. 30 by 40 inches (760 by 1015 mm)
    c. 36 by 48 inches (915 by 1220 mm)
    d. 30 by 48 inches (760 by 1220 mm)

28. Showers are most often used in which occupancy classifications?
    a. Institutional, Educational, and Assembly occupancies
    b. Educational, Residential, and Industrial occupancies
    c. Residential, Educational, and Assembly occupancies
    d. Assembly, Residential, and Institutional occupancies

29. Which of the following statements about bathing facilities is correct?
    a. The codes require the height of the walls surrounding the shower to be a minimum of 80 inches (2030 mm) above the shower drain.
    b. A curb at a shower stall cannot be higher than 0.25 inch (6.4 mm).
    c. A unisex bathing facility must include a lavatory and a water closet in addition to the bathtub or shower.
    d. An accessible lavatory is never allowed within the clear floor space of a roll-in shower.

30. The International Symbol of Accessibility should be included on a sign when it is posted at which of the following locations?
    a. On the door of an accessible toilet stall
    b. At the entrance to an accessible toilet facility
    c. At the entrance to a nonaccessible toilet facility
    d. All of the above

31. Why are suspended ceiling systems often used in conjunction with mechanical systems?
    a. They provide easy access to return ducts.
    b. They allow access to fire dampers.
    c. They help create a shaft plenum.
    d. All of the above

32. Which of the following does *not* affect the cooling load of a space?
    a. Window treatments
    b. Light fixtures
    c. People
    d. All of the above affect the cooling load

33. When designing a mechanical system, which of the following scenarios would *not* typically be zoned separately from the rest of the space?
    a. The main conference room in a large law firm
    b. A kitchen in a Mexican restaurant
    c. A small office within the interior space of an accounting firm
    d. A computer room in a high school

34. Which of the following statements about plenum air systems is correct?
    a. Certain types of wiring must be used in the plenum space.
    b. Ducts are not required in the plenum space.
    c. Some combustible materials are allowed in the plenum space.
    d. All of the above

35. When specifying products for building interiors, which of the following can affect the energy efficiency of a building?
    a. Type of lavatory faucet
    b. Type of thermostat
    c. Type of window treatment
    d. All of the above

CHAPTER 8: Electrical and Communication Requirements

1. The *National Electrical Code* is the most used electrical code in the United States.

     True/False

2. Most occupancy classifications require noncombustible electrical cables to be installed.   **True/False**

3. Outlet boxes are electrical boxes installed primarily in walls and floors.   **True/False**

4. The terms *emergency power system* and *standby power system* mean the same thing.   **True/False**

5. AFCI circuits are only required at wall receptacles in sleeping rooms.   **True/False**

6. A lock is considered to be fail-safe if the door automatically unlocks in an emergency.   **True/False**

7. Metal-clad cable is different from BX cable because it has an extra _____ wire.

8. In Residential occupancies, receptacle outlet boxes must be installed so that no point along the horizontal floor line is more than how many feet or millimeters from an outlet? _____

9. When an emergency power system takes over from the main power source during an emergency, the delay typically cannot be longer than _____ seconds.

10. When using the lighting power density tables in the energy codes and standards, you are calculating the maximum _____ allowed per square foot (square meter).

11. Communication systems are not heavily regulated by the codes because the wiring has lower _____ than electrical systems.

12. Most code requirements for electrical systems are found in which document?
    a. *NFPA 1*
    b. *NFPA 70*
    c. *NFPA 72*
    d. *NFPA 77*

13. When a designer works with an electrical engineer on a project, which of the following will typically be done by the designer?
    a. Determine the location of the electrical outlets.
    b. Determine the types of electrical cables.
    c. Determine the size of the electrical load.
    d. Determine the placement of electrical cables.

14. Which of the following may be determined by an electrical engineer?
    a. Smoke detectors
    b. Fire alarms
    c. Circuit panel size and distribution
    d. All of the above

15. Which of the following types of electrical panels is used to supply electricity to each floor within a building?
    a. Power panelboard
    b. Branch panelboard
    c. Power switchboard
    d. Service entrance switchboard

16. Which of the following statements about circuitry is *not* correct?
    a. A circuit feeds electricity to an electrical item and returns back to the panelboard.
    b. Codes limit the number of volts or amperage on a single circuit.
    c. A circuit capacity can affect the number of light fixtures on one switch.
    d. All of the above are correct.

17. Which type of cable is often used to connect light fixtures in a suspended ceiling system?
    a. Flex cable
    b. Romex cable
    c. Metal-clad cable
    d. Flat wire

18. Which of the following occupancies are typically *not* allowed by the codes to use flat wire?
    a. Assembly, Detentional, and Educational occupancies
    b. Educational, Residential, and Detentional occupancies
    c. Health Care, Educational, and Residential occupancies
    d. Health Care, Educational, and Mercantile occupancies

19. Which type of cabling is limited mostly to Residential occupancies?
    a. Romex cable
    b. Flex cable
    c. Metal-clad cable
    d. Flat wire cable

20. Which of the following statements about conduit is *not* correct?
    a. Conduit is always made of metal.
    b. A conduit can carry multiple wires.
    c. Conduit can act as a ground.
    d. All of the above are correct.

21. When an electrical cable passes through a fire barrier, the codes typically require the use of which of the following?
    a. Smokestop
    b. Fire damper
    c. Cover plate
    d. Firestop

22. If an electrical device passes through a wall assembly, what is the maximum open space allowed around the device?
    a. $\frac{3}{8}$ inch (9.6 mm)
    b. $\frac{1}{4}$ inch (6.4 mm)
    c. $\frac{1}{8}$ inch (3.1 mm)
    d. $\frac{1}{16}$ inch (1.6 mm)

23. Which of the following components is used when you want to terminate electrical wires for future use?
    a. Conduit body
    b. Junction box
    c. Receptacle outlet
    d. None of the above

24. To make a wall outlet accessible, the bottom of the outlet box must be mounted a minimum of how far from the floor?
    a. 12 inches (305 mm)
    b. 15 inches (380 mm)
    c. 20 inches (510 mm)
    d. 24 inches (610 mm)

25. Which of the following statements about light fixtures is *not* correct?
    a. All tested light fixtures are allowed in a fire-rated ceiling assembly.
    b. All light fixtures must be placed to allow easy access for future repairs and wire changes.
    c. Only labeled light fixtures can be installed on the interior of a building.
    d. All of the above are correct.

26. In which of the following situations would a GFCI outlet *not* be required?
    a. An outlet adjacent to a dwelling unit lavatory
    b. A general wall outlet in a public toilet facility
    c. An outlet adjacent to a dwelling unit wet bar
    d. A general wall outlet in a dwelling unit kitchen

27. Which of the following electrical code and accessibility requirements is correct?
    a. Hanging (pendant) light fixtures are not allowed in bathing rooms.
    b. The size of an electrical box in a rated wall is typically limited to 16 square inches (0.0103 sm).
    c. Wall sconces deeper than 4 inches (100 mm) must be mounted more than 54 inches (1370 mm) above the floor.
    d. All of the above are correct.

28. Which of the following statements about an emergency power system is *not* correct?
    a. Exit signs are often connected to an emergency power system.
    b. Artificial lighting must be present in exit discharges at all times.
    c. Emergency lighting must typically last at least $1\frac{1}{2}$ hours after power failure.
    d. All of the above are correct.

29. Which of the following does *not* affect the energy efficiency of a building?
    a. Dual switching
    b. Light fixture placement
    c. Automatic lighting shut-off
    d. All of the above affect the energy efficiency of a building.

30. Energy-efficiency requirements for building interiors can be found in which document?
    a. *ASHRAE 189.1*
    b. *ASHRAE/IESNA 90.1*
    c. *IECC*
    d. All of the above are correct.

31. Which of the following occupancies is usually required by the codes and the *ADA Standards* to have an assistive listening system?
    a. Assembly occupancy
    b. Health Care occupancy
    c. Industrial occupancy
    d. Educational occupancy

32. Which of the following are all considered part of the communication system?
    a. Intercoms, cable television, damper system
    b. Fire alarms, thermostat control, background music
    c. Intercoms, security, fire alarms
    d. Security, damper system, cable television

33. Which of the following statements is *not* correct?
    a. Most communication rooms must be separated from the rest of the building by rated assemblies.
    b. Communication rooms must meet requirements found in the *NEC* and other industry standards.
    c. Smaller communication and satellite rooms must meet requirements similar to communication rooms.
    d. All of the above are correct.

34. Match each of the unique characteristics on the right with the type of communication cable shown on the left.
    ___ Fiber-optic cable   a. Commonly used for video transmissions
    ___ Twisted-pair cable   b. Uses transmitters to connect users to system
    ___ Wireless   c. Bundles various types of cables into one sleeve
    ___ Zone cabling   d. Are rated by category
    ___ Circuit integrity cable   e. Provides the highest speed and capacity
    ___ Coaxial cable   f. Uses intermediate terminals in ceilings
    ___ Composite cable   g. Provides a 2-hour fire rating

35. Which of the following communication cabling requirements is correct?
    a. Low-voltage cabling run above a suspended ceiling system must be in cable trays.
    b. All old low-voltage cabling that is abandoned does not have to be removed.
    c. Low-voltage cables run in ceiling plenums must typically be rated for plenums.
    d. Electrical and low-voltage wiring are typically run together in the same conduit.

CHAPTER 9: Finish and Furniture Selection

1. A fabric will require a different test depending on whether it is used as a wallcovering or window treatment.   **True/False**

2. The *Smolder Resistance Test* is also known as the *Cigarette Ignition Test.*   **True/False**

3. If you found a used sofa, you could have it tested and use it in a space that requires its seating to pass *CAL 133.*   **True/False**

4. When wood veneer is used as an interior finish, it may have to be treated to meet code finish requirements.   **True/False**

5. Paint applied to any surface does not have to be rated because it is considered thermally thin.   **True/False**

6. As you travel through a means of egress toward the exit discharge, the required finish classes become stricter.   **True/False**

7. If a finish is not pretested, there is no way you can use it on a project.   **True/False**

8. Many of the sustainable product standards use product certifications as a benchmark to measure a product.   **True/False**

9. A fire _____ is a separate material that may be used underneath an upholstery fabric on a chair or sofa for the purpose of creating a fire barrier.

10. _____ occurs when a fire generates so much heat that the combustible materials in the room reach their ignition temperature and simultaneously ignite.

11. A(n) _____ company can add a fire retardant coating to a finish to make it more flame resistant.

12. Accessibility requirements for furniture usually apply to two types of furniture: seating and _____.

13. VOC is an acronym for volatile _____ compounds.

14. Match each test name on the left with the number designation shown on the right. Fill in the appropriate letter on the lines shown.
     __ *Pill Test*   **a.** *NFPA 265*
     __ *Steiner Tunnel Test*   **b.** *16 CFR 1630*
     __ *Vertical Flame Test*   **c.** *ASTM E648*
     __ *Radiant Panel Test*   **d.** *NFPA 260*
     __ *Room Corner Test*   **e.** *NFPA 701*
     __ *Toxicity Test*   **f.** *NFPA 269*
     __ *Smolder Resistance Test*   **g.** *16 CFR 1632*
     __ *Mattress Test*   **h.** *ASTM E84*

15. Which of the following finish tests is a rated test and *not* a pass/fail test?
    a. *Vertical Flame Test*
    b. *Radiant Panel Test*
    c. *Room Corner Test*
    d. *Pill Test*

16. Which of the following tests is required for mattresses used in certain Institutional occupancies?
    a. *16 CFR 1632*
    b. *CAL 117*
    c. *ASTM E1590*
    d. *NFPA 272*

17. Which of the following tests would *not* typically be used on the upholstery of a chair?
    a. *Steiner Tunnel Test*
    b. *CAL 133*
    c. *Radiant Panel Test*
    d. *Smolder Resistance Test*

18. The *Pitts Test* is typically used to test which of the following?
    a. Finishes
    b. Mattresses
    c. Conduit
    d. All of the above

19. Which of the following does *not* typically affect the finish test required on a project?
    a. The size of the building
    b. Where the finish is applied
    c. The type of occupancy classification
    d. The jurisdiction of the project

20. Which of the following statements about *CAL 133* is correct?
    a. The test results in a class rating.
    b. The aim of the test is to eliminate the flashover that occurs in the second phase of a fire.
    c. It is a test required by the building codes.
    d. All of the above are correct.

21. Which of the following is *not* a *Room Corner Test*?
    a. *UL 1715*
    b. *NFPA 265*
    c. *NFPA 286*
    d. *NFPA 253*

22. A fabric is considered flame resistant if it does what?
    a. Resists catching on fire
    b. Chars instead of burns
    c. Terminates the flame after the ignition source is removed
    d. All of the above

23. Which of the following finish tests would be used on a tufted fabric applied to a wall?
    a. *Room Corner Test*
    b. *Steiner Tunnel Test*
    c. *Radiant Panel Test*
    d. *Smolder Resistance Test*

24. Which of the following finish tests uses a cigarette and measures the char mark created to determine if a fabric passes or fails?
    a. *Smolder Resistance Test*
    b. *Vertical Flame Test*
    c. *Radiant Panel Test*
    d. *Pill Test*

25. Which of the following finish tests measures both how fast a flame will spread and how much smoke is created?
    a. *Toxicity Test*
    b. *Steiner Tunnel Test*
    c. *Room Corner Test*
    d. *Radiant Panel Test*

26. The *Life Safety Code* requires wall base that is 6 inches (152 mm) or less to meet the requirements of which of the following tests?
    a. *Radiant Panel Test*
    b. *Pill Test*
    c. *Steiner Tunnel Test*
    d. *Room Corner Test*

27. Which of the following finish tests is typically used on vertical finishes exposed to air on both sides?
    a. *CAL 116*
    b. *UL 723*
    c. *NFPA 701*
    d. *ASTM E648*

28. Why would you first have a sample tested before having a fire retardant finish added to the fabric for a drapery treatment?
    a. The fabric is a special blend and you want to make sure the fabric will not shrink.
    b. The fabric has a texture and you want to make sure the texture will not flatten.
    c. The fabric has a bold pattern and you want to make sure the colors will not bleed into each other.
    d. All of the above

29. Which of the following occupancy classifications tend to have the strictest finish and furniture code requirements?
    a. Residential, Health Care, and Assembly occupancies
    b. Educational, Assembly, and Health Care occupancies
    c. Detentional/Correctional, Assembly, and Educational occupancies
    d. Health Care, Detentional/Correctional, and Residential occupancies

30. Which of the following statements is *not* correct?
    a. A building with an automatic sprinkler system will not typically require rated finishes.
    b. When a finish is applied to furring strips, the intervening spaces must either be filled with a fire-rated material or be fire blocked.
    c. Mirrors are not allowed on or adjacent to an exit door.
    d. Glass used as an interior finish will be required to meet safety glazing requirements if used in certain locations.

31. Which type of finish may be affected by the "percent rule"?
    a. Wall hanging, heavy timber, crown molding
    b. Cellular plastic, furring strips, wall hanging
    c. Crown molding, non-tested finish, wall hangings
    d. Non-tested finish, cellular plastic, heavy timber

32. Which of the following would typically have the strictest finish requirements?
    a. Exit stair
    b. Executive office
    c. Exit access corridor
    d. Conference room

33. For a worksurface or countertop to be considered accessible, what clear kneespace height is required?
    a. 24 inches (610 mm)
    b. 27 inches (685 mm)
    c. 28 inches (710 mm)
    d. 30 inches (760 mm)

34. Which of the following flooring situations would be least likely to meet typical accessibility requirements?
    a. A detectable warning in the floor at the top of a ramp
    b. A carpet installed with a thin, double-stick pad
    c. A slip-resistant floor finish in a shower room
    d. A marble floor butting up to a carpet with no pad

35. The *Smolder Resistance Tests* were developed specifically to test which of the following?
    a. Fabrics
    b. Mock-ups
    c. Drapes
    d. Foams

36. Which of the following statements about the symbols created by the Association for Contract Textiles (ACT) is *not* correct?
    a. They indicate a textile's characteristics regarding colorfastness, abrasion, flammability, and other physical properties.
    b. They set standards for upholstery, wallcoverings, upholstered walls, drapery, and furniture.
    c. They indicate the standard test the item must meet in order to bear the symbol.
    d. All of the above are correct.

37. Because the designer can be held liable for a project even after it is completed, which of the following is *not* a good finish and furniture selection practice for liability reasons?
    a. Strictly following the requirements of the project's jurisdiction
    b. Keeping all your research organized and with the rest of the project information
    c. Making photocopies of all code sections that apply to your project
    d. Maintaining a code checklist indicating the standards used for each project

38. Sustainable product certification programs are available for which types of interior products?
    a. Fabrics and upholsteries
    b. Flooring and adhesives
    c. Furniture and components
    d. All of the above

CHAPTER 10: Code Officials and the Code Process

1. A permit must be obtained for all interior projects.   **True/False**

2. A code requirement can have more than one interpretation.   **True/False**

3. When a code discrepancy is brought to the Board of Appeals, the board has the authority to waive that code requirement.   **True/False**

4. During the preliminary design, you should typically get the appropriate federal agency to review your plans for compliance with federal laws.   **True/False**

5. A number of jurisdictions have instituted green building programs, many of which require the use of a green rating system.   **True/False**

6. An authority having jurisdiction can include a code jurisdiction, a code _____, and a code _____.

7. A(n) _____ must be clearly posted at the job site during construction.

8. Code research should typically begin during the _____ phase of the design process.

9. A permit is typically obtained from the codes department by a(n) _____.

10. Code research should be documented in project files, construction drawings, and/or _____.

11. Which of the following code officials will review your construction drawings during both the preliminary review and the final review?
    a. Plans examiner and fire marshal
    b. Building inspector and plans examiner
    c. Building inspector and fire marshal
    d. Plans examiner and building examiner

12. What is the first step in determining which codes to use on a project?
    a. To determine which edition is being used
    b. To determine in which jurisdiction the project is located
    c. To determine if any local amendments have been made
    d. To determine what is required for final code approval

13. Which of the following steps in the code process is *not* typically done by the designer?
    a. Code research
    b. Permit process
    c. Appeals process
    d. Preliminary review

14. Which of the following scenarios would typically *not* require a permit?
    a. Reconfiguring one wall to enlarge an existing office
    b. Replacing an existing HVAC system on the third floor of a building
    c. Adding a demising wall to create a new tenant space
    d. Replacing the wallpaper in a retirement center

15. A preliminary code review of your drawings should be done with a code official during which stage of the design process?
    a. Programming phase
    b. Design phase
    c. Schematic phase
    d. Construction drawing phase

16. Which of the following would be a valid reason to try to obtain an appeal for an interior project?
    a. The conditions in an existing building will not allow you to fully meet a code requirement.
    b. A particular code requirement is going to be very costly and you want to use an alternate solution.
    c. You and the code official(s) in your jurisdiction cannot agree on an interpretation of one of the codes required for your project.
    d. All of the above

17. Which of the following statements is true?
    a. When the Board of Appeals grants your appeal, it can be used on future projects as long as the same code scenario occurs.
    b. If you take your drawings through the preliminary review process, you will be allowed to skip the permit review process.
    c. A tenant can occupy a space if a Temporary Certificate of Occupancy has been issued by a code official.
    d. All of the above are true.

18. When a jurisdiction requires the use of a green building program, which of the following should you do when designing your project?
    a. Work closely with the local code official.
    b. Use LEED as the green rating system.
    c. Hire a third-party consultant to do all of the inspections.
    d. All of the above

19. Which of the following is *not* a typical code inspection required on an interior project?
    a. Final inspection
    b. Footing inspection
    c. Framing inspection
    d. Penetration inspection

20. Why does a code official inspect a project during construction?
    a. To make sure the work complies with the codes
    b. To ensure that a Certificate of Occupancy can be issued
    c. To guarantee that the work matches the construction documents
    d. All of the above

21. Which of the following would *not* be a reason to use a performance code in a project?
    a. The client wants to avoid paying for the addition of a fire wall, so you want to use an alternate wall assembly.
    b. A new sustainable product just became available and you want to use it in place of a material suggested by the codes.
    c. You want to build all the corridor walls out of transparent plastic but some of the walls are required to be fire rated and you have an alternate solution.
    d. An existing building will not allow you to meet all the typical means of egress requirements without costly changes, so you want to enhance the extinguishing system.

22. Which of the following statements about the documentation of performance requirements is *not* correct?
   a. The performance-related requirements should be clearly delineated from the perspective code requirements.
   b. During plan review, the documentation is always reviewed by an outside consultant known as a contract reviewer.
   c. The documentation will typically include more than just the construction drawings and specifications.
   d. It will often require a review process separate from the prescriptive code part of the project.

23. A jurisdiction determines which of the following aspects of the permit review?
   a. Who can submit drawings
   b. Which types of drawings are required
   c. The cost of permit fees
   d. All of the above

24. Whom should you ask to determine which codes are required in a jurisdiction?
   a. The code official in the jurisdiction of your office
   b. The code official in the jurisdiction of your project
   c. The client of your project
   d. The licensed contractor working on your project

SECTION 3

STUDY PROBLEMS

☐ CHAPTER 1: About the Codes

PROBLEM 1

Chapter 1 discusses the main code organizations, standards organizations, and federal agencies as they relate to interior projects. Fill in as many as you can remember in the spaces provided. Show full names and acronyms.

Code Organizations:

1. _____

2. _____

Standards Organizations:

1. _____

2. _____

3. _____

4. _____

5. _____

Federal Agencies:

1. _____

2. _____

3. _____

4. _____

5. _____

PROBLEM 2

In the spaces provided, fill in the full code, standard name, or federal regulation based on the acronym shown.

ABA_____

ADA_____

EPAct_____

FHA_____

IBC_____

ICC A117.1 _____

ICCPC_____

IEBC_____

IECC_____

IFC_____

IGCC_____

IMC_____

IPC_____

IRC_____

LSC_____

NEC_____

NFPA 1 _____

UMC_____

UPC_____

CHAPTER 2: Occupancy Classifications and Loads

PROBLEM 1

Refer to the chart, "Comparison of Occupancy Classifications," in Appendix A.1 (or Figure 2.2 in the *Guidebook*) for this problem. This chart lists all the occupancy classifications for the *International Building Code (IBC)* and the NFPA codes such as the *Life Safety Code (LSC)*.

Based on this chart, answer the following questions concerning occupancy classifications. Write your answers in the spaces provided.

a. If you were asked to design the interior of a prison located in a jurisdiction using the *IBC*, which occupancy classification would you use?_____

b. Using the *IBC* and the *LSC*, which occupancy classifications would you use if you were asked to redesign the interior of a hotel? List the appropriate classification for each.

   IBC:_____

   LSC:_____

c. A client asks you to select finishes for a nightclub that he owns. Based on the *LSC*, what additional information do you need in order to determine the correct occupancy classification?_____

d. If you are designing the interior of a large assisted living facility that accommodates 150 residents and you are using the *IBC*, which occupancy classification would you use?_____

   Why?_____

   _____

   _____

e. If you are selecting finishes for the same assisted living facility using the *LSC*, which occupancy classification would you use?_____

   Why?_____

   _____

   _____

PROBLEM 2

Refer to *International Building Code* Table 1004.1.2, "Maximum Floor Area Allowances per Occupant," in Appendix A.2 (or Figure 2.8 in the *Guidebook*) for this problem.

Based on *IBC* Table 1004.1.2, determine the occupant load for the floor plan shown in Figure 2.1. The plan is for a retail clothing store on the first floor (at grade level) of a strip mall. Use the occupant load formula to determine the occupant load for this store; write your answer in the space provided. (The metric conversion variable is given at the bottom of the code table.)

Occupant load of Figure 2.1= _____

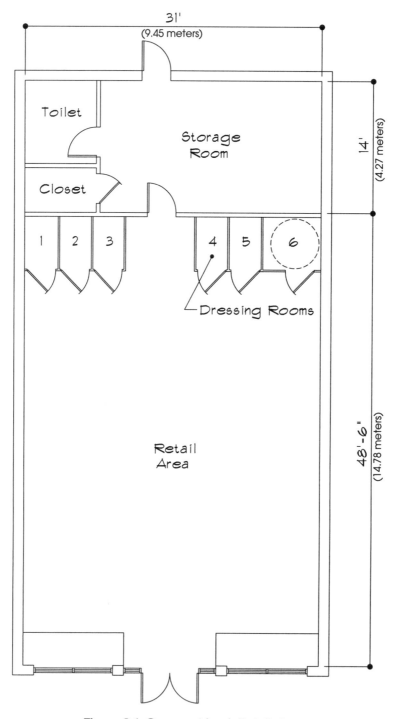

Figure 2.1. Occupant load: Retail store.

PROBLEM 3

Refer to *International Building Code* Table 1004.1.2, "Maximum Floor Area Allowances per Occupant," in Appendix A.2 (or Figure 2.8 in the *Guidebook*), and use what you know about the codes to answer this problem.

a. Figure 2.2 shows the floor plans of four single-story buildings. In which plan could the Storage (S) occupancy or use be considered an accessory to the main occupancy classification? Write the letter of the plan selected in the space provided and explain your answer._____

   Explain: _____

   _____

b. Based on *IBC* Table 1004.1.2, determine the total occupant load for the building in Plan A of Figure 2.2 with the Educational and Storage uses. The Educational (E) use is primarily classrooms. Write your answer in the space provided. (The metric conversion variable is given at the bottom of the code table.)

   Occupant load of Plan A in Figure 2.2 = _____

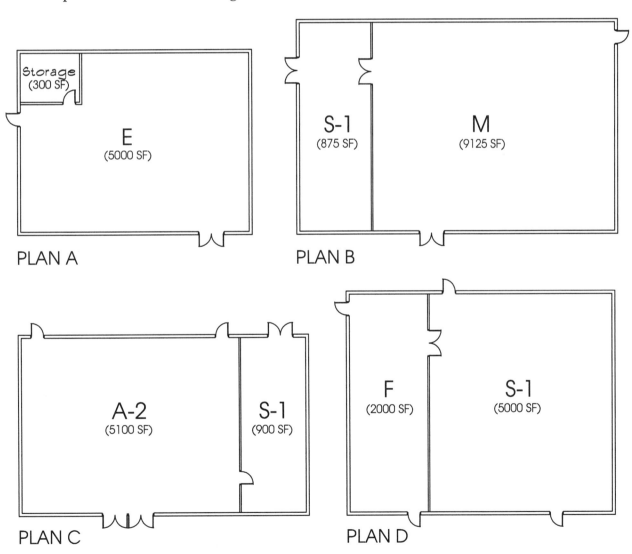

Figure 2.2. More than one occupancy: Single-story buildings. (1 square foot = 0.0929 square meter)

PROBLEM 4

The schematic design for the building shown in Figure 2.3 is a college building that includes a Meeting Room, Library, and Administrative Offices. It also includes toilet facilities and a small amount of storage for users of the Meeting Room and the Library. The area in the center of the building, noted on the plan as the Central Hall, contains tables and chairs and is used as a study or eating space. It also allows for the egress path from the different spaces. Using what you know about occupant loads, answer the following questions about the occupant loads and means of egress requirements for this design. Write your answer in the space provided. (The metric conversion variable is given at the bottom of the code table.)

a. What is the occupant load of the entire building in Figure 2.3? _____

b. The means of egress (exits) from the Central Hall in Figure 2.3 must be designed to accommodate what occupant load? _____

c. Is the number of exits shown from each of the spaces in Figure 2.3 sufficient for the occupant load they serve? Write yes or no in the space provided and explain your answer. _____

Explain:_____

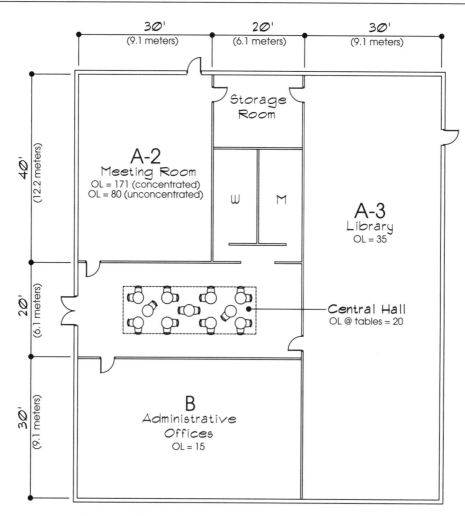

Figure 2.3 More than one occupancy: College building.

PROBLEM 5

Refer to *International Building Code)* Table 1004.1.2, "Maximum Floor Area Allowances per Occupant," in Appendix A.2 (or Figure 2.8 in the *Guidebook*) for this problem.

a. Based on *IBC* Table 1004.1.2, determine the occupant load for the church in the floor plan shown in Figure 2.4. The seating shown consists of continuous wooden pews bolted to the floor. As shown on the floor plan, all pews are the same size: 14'-6" (4419.6 mm) long. This includes the 3-inch (76.2-mm) wide arms on each end. Write your answer in the space provided.

Occupant load of Figure 2.4 = _____

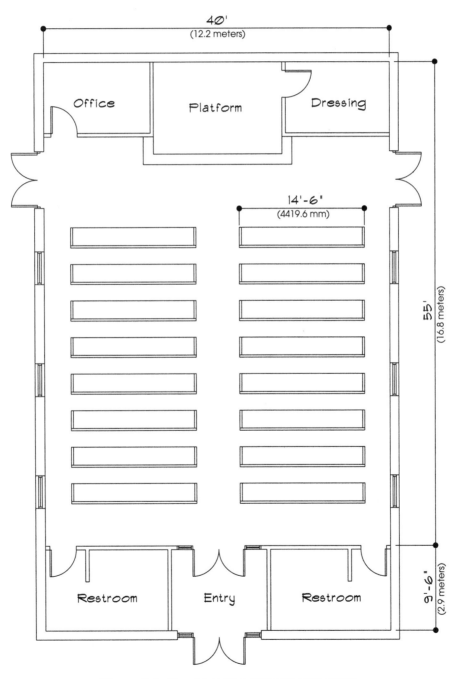

Figure 2.4. Fixed seating: Church with pews.

b. Using the same floor plan in Figure 2.4, determine the occupant load if this were an auditorium with a row of seating that has dividing arms. An example of this seating arrangement is shown in Figure 2.5. A dividing arm separates each seat, and eight people can sit in each pew. Write your answer in the space provided.

Occupant load of Figure 2.4 with dividing arms = _____

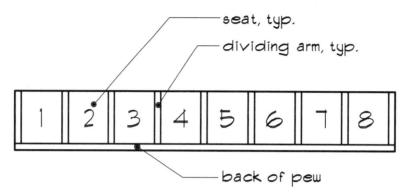

Figure 2.5. Fixed seating: Divided pews.

PROBLEM 6

Refer to *International Building Code* Table 1004.1.2, "Maximum Floor Area Allowances per Occupant," in Appendix A.2 (or Figure 2.8 in the *Guidebook*) for this problem.

A developer recently purchased a vacant building, an old high school that closed more than 10 years ago. You are working with a team to help the developer determine how to develop the building. There are two floors, each floor with 4600 square feet (427.34 sm), for a total of 9200 gross square feet (854.7 sm.) Using the occupant load formula and *IBC* Table 1004.1.2, determine which of the following three scenarios will be allowed by the codes. Give a yes or no answer, and explain how you obtained your answer in the spaces provided. (The metric conversion variable is given at the bottom of the code table.)

a. The developer is considering an apartment complex. She wants to divide the building into multiple units. She has assumed the total occupant load for the building to be 54. Based on the actual occupant load capacity for the building, will this work?_____

Explain: _____

_____

_____

b. The developer is considering turning the building into a retirement center that provides minimum health services. She plans to house 62 tenants and expects 8 full-time employees. Based on the occupant load, will this work? _____

Explain:_____

_____

_____

c. The developer is also considering a two-story retail center with stores open to the public on both floors. She expects an occupant load of 125 on the first floor and 85 on the second floor. Based on the occupant load, will this work? _____

Explain: _____

_____

_____

CHAPTER 3: Construction Types and Building Sizes

PROBLEM 1

Refer to *International Building Code* Table 601, "Fire-Resistance Rating Requirements for Building Elements," in Appendix A.3 (or Figure 3.1 in the *Guidebook*) for this problem.

Based on *IBC* Table 601, answer each of the following questions. Fill in your answers in the spaces provided.

a. What do the designations of A and B indicate in this chart?_____
_____

b. What is the typical fire resistance rating for columns that are part of the structural frame in a Type VA building?_____

c. What is the typical fire resistance rating for an interior bearing wall within a Type IIA building?_____

d. Which construction type requires a 2-hour fire rating for its floor construction?

_____

e. According to this table, which structure or building element does not typically require a fire rating? _____

PROBLEM 2

Refer to *International Building Code* Table 503, "Allowable Building Height and Areas," in Appendix A.4 (or Figure 3.4 in the *Guidebook*) for this problem, as well as the chart "Comparison of Occupancy Classifications" in Appendix A.1 (or Figure 2.2 in the *Guidebook*), if required.

Using *IBC* Table 503, determine which of the following scenarios would be allowed by the *IBC*. Give a yes or no answer, then explain how you obtained this answer in the spaces provided. Be specific, using your knowledge of occupancy classifications and the information shown in the code table. (A multiplier for metric conversion is given at the bottom of the table.)

a. An existing nonsprinklered building with a construction type of Type IIIB has two floors with 17,500 square feet (1626 sm) per floor. Can this building be converted into a hotel?_____

   Explain:_____

   _____

   _____

b. A local developer is planning to develop a series of townhouses. Some will be three stories and others will be four stories. They will all be Type VB construction. The typical first floor will be 3625 square feet (337 sm); the second floor will be 2880 square feet (268 sm); and the third and fourth floors will be 1000 square feet (93 sm) each. Can this be developed as planned according to the *IBC*?_____

   Explain:_____

   _____

   _____

c. Your client has found a potential building for the relocation of a low-hazard factory use. The space is the first floor of an existing two-story building, which has a construction type of Type IIIB. Each floor in this building has 19,250 gross square feet (1788 sm). The client expects to expand to have 100 employees. If the occupant load factor for this factory is 100 gross square feet (9.3 sm) per person, will this space work?_____

   Explain:_____

   _____

   _____

PROBLEM 1

Using the stair diagram shown in Figure 4.1, fill in the typical code requirements for each of the following in the spaces provided. Be sure to indicate whether you are using inches or millimeters. Add the words *minimum* and *maximum* where applicable.

A. Riser height: _____

B. Tread depth: _____

C. Nosing projection: _____

D. Stairway rise without landing: _____

E. Height of handrail: _____

F. Top handrail extension: _____

G. Bottom handrail extension: _____

H. Diameter of Type I circular handrail: _____

I. Minimum headroom height: _____

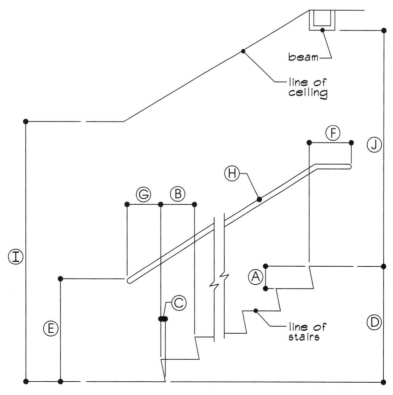

Figure 4.1. Section/Elevation of stairs.

PROBLEM 2

The diagram shown in Figure 4.2 is a line drawing that represents a section of a fully sprinklered high-rise building. It is a new building, with the first floor at grade level. You are given the occupant load and the use group for each floor. Use the diagram and the information you are given to answer the questions in this two-part problem.

a. Use the occupant load for each floor shown in Figure 4.2, the following chart, and your knowledge of the means of egress codes to determine the number of exits for each floor. List the quantities in the space provided.

FLOOR 8	**Penthouse Apartment** OL = 435
FLOOR 7	**Executive Offices** OL = 775
FLOOR 6	**Office Spaces** OL = 450
FLOOR 5	**Office Spaces** OL = 990
FLOOR 4	**Office Spaces** OL = 1525
FLOOR 3	**Office Spaces** OL = 960
FLOOR 2	**Wholesale Retail Shops** OL = 475
FLOOR 1	**Restaurant** OL = 360
BASEMENT	**Storage** OL = 51

Figure 4.2. Number of exits: High-rise building (sprinklered building).

Occupant Load per Story/Floor	Minimum Number of Exits
1–500	2
500–1000	3
Over 1000	4

Basement: _____
First Floor: _____
Second Floor: _____
Third Floor: _____
Fourth Floor: _____
Fifth Floor: _____
Sixth Floor: _____
Seventh Floor: _____
Eighth Floor: _____

b. Refer to *International Building Code (IBC)* Table 1015.1, "Spaces with One Exit or Exit Access Doorway" and Table 1021.2(2), "Stories with One Exit or Access to One Exit for Other Occupancies" in Appendix A.5 (or Figure 4.17 in the *Guidebook*), and Table 1016.1, "Exit Access Travel Distance" in Appendix A.6 (or Figure 4.24 in the *Guidebook*) for this part of the problem.

Answer the following questions using the information shown in the diagram in Figure 4.2 and these code tables. (Be sure to refer to the notes at the bottom of the code tables.) Note which code table was used to determine your answer. Write your answers in the spaces provided. (A multiplier for metric conversion is given at the bottom of the tables.)

1. What is the maximum travel distance allowed on the first floor in Figure 4.2?

   Distance:_____

   Code Table:_____

2. If this were a fully sprinklered single-story office building with 35 occupants and 1 exit, what would be the maximum travel distance allowed?

   Distance:_____

   Code Table:_____

3. What is the maximum travel distance allowed on the second floor in Figure 4.2?

   Distance:_____

   Code Table:_____

4. If these retail shops were located in a two-story building with one exit, what would be the allowable travel distance?

   Distance:_____

   Code Table:_____

5. What is the maximum travel distance allowed on the third through seventh floors in Figure 4.2?

   Distance:_____

   Code Table:_____

PROBLEM 3

Refer to NFPA *Life Safety Code (LSC)* Table 7.3.3.1, "Capacity Factors" in Appendix A.7 (or Figure 4.19 in the *Guidebook*) for this problem.

Figure 4.3 is a floor plan of the third floor in a four-story building. The third floor has just been totally renovated and a new automatic sprinkler system was installed. Four new tenants plan to occupy the floor. All the tenants are considered Business (B) occupancies. Use the width variables from *LSC* Table 7.3.3.1 and your knowledge of minimum means of egress widths to answer the following three-part problem. Write your answers in the spaces provided. (Indicate whether you are using inches or millimeters.)

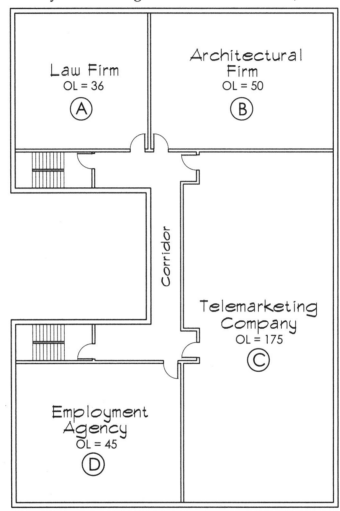

Figure 4.3. Exit widths: Multi-tenant building (third floor) (sprinklered building).

a. What is the total exit width required for the telemarketing company in Space C?_____

   If the space requires two exits, how wide does each exit or exit door have to be?_____

   Why?_____

b. What is the total exit width required for each exit stair?_____

   Why?_____

c. What is the minimum exit width required for the exit access corridor?_____

   Why?_____

PROBLEM 4

Figure 4.4 shows a table and chair layout for a training room. (It is drawn to scale at 1/8" = 1'-0".) Use a straightedge and an architectural scale with this floor plan to determine the answers to the following questions. Using the information given here and the floor plan, determine the minimum required width between the edges of each table at the aisle accessways indicated.

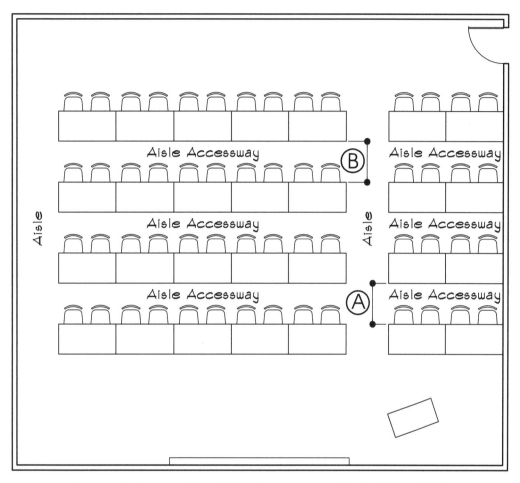

Figure 4.4. Access aisle widths: Training room (Scale: 1/8" = 1'-0").

Aisle Accessway Length	Minimum Width
< 6 feet (1829 mm)	None
6–12 feet (1829–3658 mm)	12 inches (305 mm)
12–30 feet (3658–9144 mm)	12 inches + 0.05 (x−12 feet)
	or
	305 mm + 12.7((x − 3658 mm) / 305)

a. What is the required minimum distance between the tables at Aisle Accessway A?_____
    Explain:_____

b. What is the required minimum distance between the tables at Aisle Accessway B?_____
    Explain:_____

PROBLEM 5

Figure 4.5 is a floor plan of a doctor's office in a tenant space on the ground floor of a multi-story building. The building is nonsprinklered. (It is drawn to scale at 1/8" = 1'-0". The only exit from the space is in the waiting area. Use a straightedge and an architectural scale with this floor plan to determine the answers to the following questions. Write your answers in the spaces provided and show how you obtained your answers directly on the floor plan, drawing lines and dimensions where necessary. Label any lines you draw with the corresponding letter of the question or use a different color pencil or highlighter for each question. Refer to *LSC* Table 1014.2, "Common Path of Egress Travel" in Appendix A.8 (or Figure 4.27 in the *Guidebook*) for this problem.

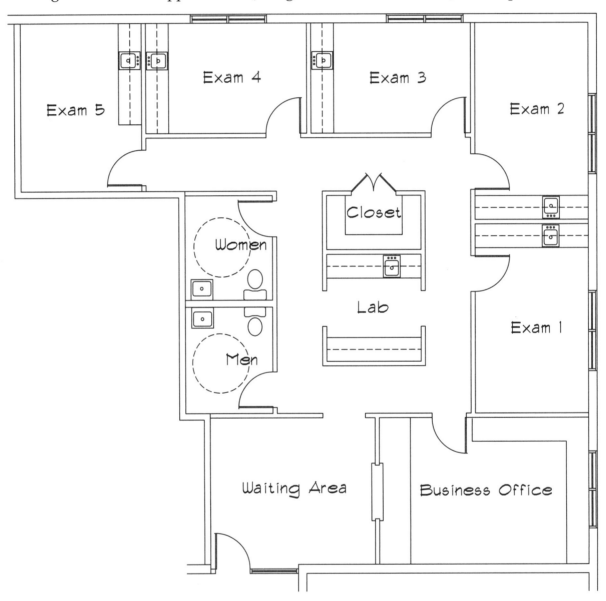

Figure 4.5. Travel distances: Doctor's office (nonsprinklered building) (Scale: 1/8" = 1'-0").

a. If this space were required to have two exits, what would be the minimum required distance between the two exits?_____

Explain:_____

_____

_____

b. What is the longest travel distance in this space?_____

c. Is there a dead-end corridor in this space?_____ If so, how long is it?_____
Is it allowed?_____

Explain:_____

d. Is there a common path of egress travel in this space?_____ If so, where is it located?
_____

How long is it? _____ Is this distance allowable by the code?

CHAPTER 5: Fire and Smoke Resistant Assemblies

PROBLEM 1

Refer to *International Building Code (IBC)* Table 508.4, "Required Separation of Occupancies (Hours)" in Appendix A.9 (or Figure 5.6 in the *Guidebook*); *IBC* Table 509, "Incidental Uses" in Appendix A.10 (or Figure 5.8 in the *Guidebook*); *IBC* Table 1018.1, "Corridor Fire-Resistance Rating" in Appendix A.11 (or Figure 5.11 in the *Guidebook*); and *IBC* Table 716.5, "Opening Fire Protection Assemblies, Ratings and Markings" in Appendix A.12 (or Figure 5.12 in the *Guidebook*) for this problem. (Use the "Comparison of Occupancy Classifications" chart in Appendix A.1 as required.)

Figure 5.1 is a floor plan of the eighth floor in a 10-story nonsprinklered office building. It shows the layout of the building core and five tenant spaces, as well as the interior of one tenant space. The tenants are either Business (B) or Mercantile (M) occupancies, as shown on the plan. The legend at the bottom of the floor plan indicates the name of each labeled room or space. Specific wall assemblies on the floor plan are labeled with a circled *letter* designation, and certain doors (or opening protectives) are labeled with a circled *number* designation.

Based on the floor plan, the *IBC* tables mentioned earlier, and your knowledge of the codes, first determine the fire resistance rating for each of the labeled wall assemblies. Then, for each of the labeled opening protectives, determine the fire protection rating of the door assembly. Also note any situations where an automatic extinguishing system could be substituted for a rated wall. Write your answers and the code table used in the spaces provided here. If a rating is not required for a particular item, write "no rating" in the space provided; or if a code table is not used, write "no table" in the space provided.

Hourly Fire Resistance Rating of Wall Assemblies:

A. Rating:_____ Code Table:_____

B. Rating:_____ Code Table:_____

C. Rating:_____ Code Table:_____

D. Rating:_____ Code Table:_____

E. Rating:_____ Code Table:_____

F. Rating:_____ Code Table:_____

G. Rating:_____ Code Table:_____

H. Rating:_____ Code Table:_____

Hourly Fire Protection Rating of Opening Protectives:

1. Rating:_____ Code Table:_____

2. Rating:_____ Code Table:_____

3. Rating: _____ Code Table:_____

4. Rating:_____ Code Table:_____

5. Rating:_____ Code Table:_____

6. Rating:_____ Code Table:_____

7. Rating:_____ Code Table:_____

8. Rating:_____ Code Table:_____

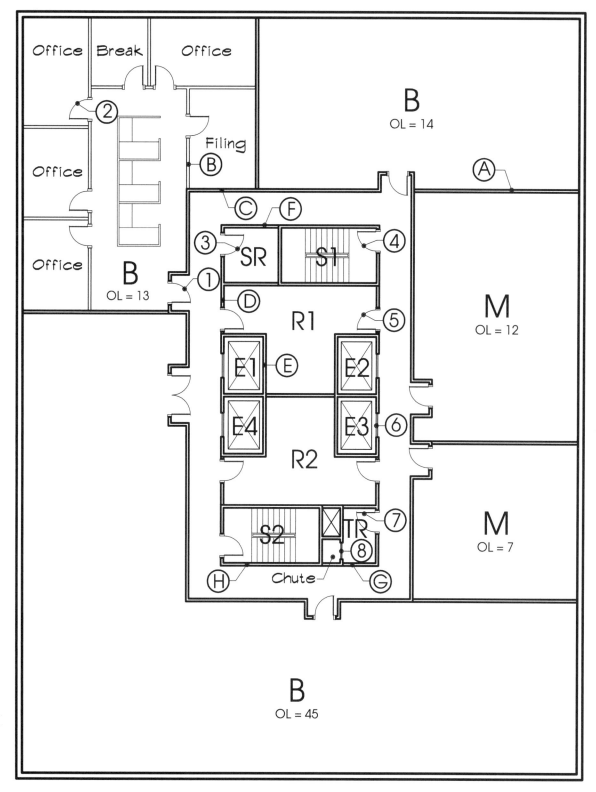

Figure 5.1. Fire ratings: Office building, eighth floor (nonsprinklered building).

E = Elevator   SR = Storage Room (150 SF or 14 SM)
R = Restroom   TR = Trash Room (120 SF or 11.1 SM)
S = Exit Stair   OL = Occupant Load

PROBLEM 2

Refer to *International Building Code (IBC)* Table 509, "Incidental Uses," in Appendix A.10 (or Figure 5.8 in the *Guidebook*) for this problem.

   IBC Table 509 provides specific fire separation and protection requirements for special rooms and spaces within a building. Based on this *IBC* table, answer the following questions. Write your answers in the spaces provided.

a. What is the fire rating of a wall in a collection room for soiled linen with an area of 250 square feet (23 sm) in the basement of a hotel?_____ Is an automatic sprinkler system required?_____

b. Is a fire resistance–rated partition required in a 110-square-foot (10.2-sm) storage room located in a high school?_____

c. Can you substitute an automatic sprinkler system for the 1-hour fire resistance–rated partitions around waste and linen collection rooms in a hospital?_____ Explain:_____

d. Does a science lab in a high school require a fire rating? If so, can a sprinkler system be used instead?_____

e. Which of the listed incidental accessory occupancies are determined by their size, not just what is contained in them?_____

☐ CHAPTER 6: Fire Protection Systems

PROBLEM 1

Automatic sprinkler systems can greatly enhance the fire protection of a building. They can also help to eliminate or reduce other code requirements, as the codes allow automatic sprinkler systems as a "trade-off" for other code requirements. Quite a few of these trade-offs are discussed in Chapter 5 and Chapter 6 of the *Guidebook*.

   List six trade-offs that would affect the interior of a building. Write the answers in the spaces provided here.

1. _____

2. _____

3. _____

4. _____

5. _____

6. _____

PROBLEM 2

Figure 6.1 contains diagrams of five typical sprinkler-head orientations. Identify each type.

A. _____

B. _____

C. _____

D. _____

E. _____

F. _____

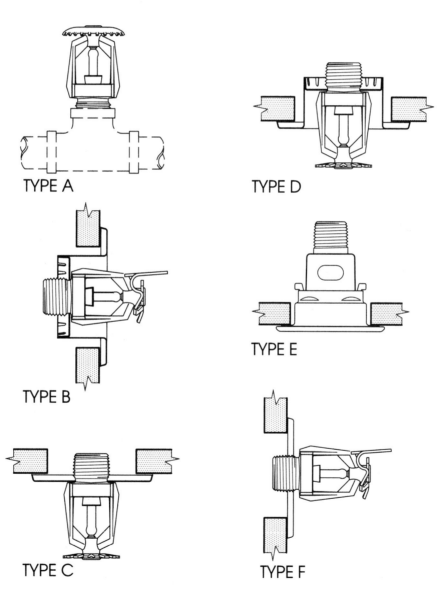

Figure 6.1. Orientation of sprinkler heads.
(Line drawings reprinted with permission from Viking Group [www.vikingcorp.com].)

CHAPTER 7: Plumbing and Mechanical Requirements

PROBLEM 1

The diagram shown in Figure 7.1 represents three elevations of a typical accessible single-toilet facility. The letters indicated in the diagram correspond to the letters listed here. Fill in the typical dimension as required by the current codes and accessibility standards for each of the following in the spaces provided. (Indicate the most restrictive requirement.) Be sure to indicate whether you are using inches or millimeters. Add the words *minimum* and *maximum* where applicable.

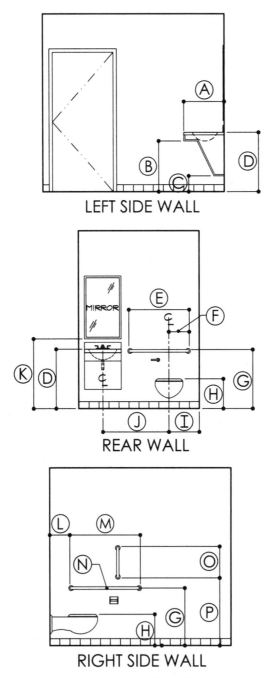

Figure 7.1. Typical accessible toilet elevations.

A. Depth of lavatory:_____

B. Height of clear kneespace:_____

C. Height of clear toespace:_____

D. Height to top of lavatory:_____

E. Length of rear grab bar:_____

F. Distance from end of rear grab bar to centerline of toilet:_____

G. Height to grab bar:_____

H. Height to top of toilet seat:_____

I. Distance from centerline of toilet to side wall:_____

J. Distance between centerline of toilet and centerline of lavatory:_____

K. Height to bottom of mirror:_____

L. Distance from rear wall to side grab bar:_____

M. Length of side grab bar:_____

N. Diameter of grab bar:_____

O. Height of vertical grab bar:_____

P. Distance from floor to bottom of vertical grab bar:_____

PROBLEM 2

Refer to *International Plumbing Code (IPC)* Table 403.1, "Minimum Number of Required Plumbing Fixtures," in Appendix A.14 (or Figure 7.1 in the *Guidebook*) for this problem.

Answer the questions to the following plumbing fixture scenarios based on your knowledge of occupancy classifications and *IPC* Table 403.1. Fill in the answers and explain how you obtained your answers in the spaces provided.

a. How many female and male water closets are required in an elementary school with a total of 820 occupants?
   Female:_____

   Male:_____

   Explain:_____

   _____

   _____

b. How many visitor and employee water closets are required in a nursing home with an occupant load of 155?_____

   Explain:_____

   _____

   _____

c. Determine the number of water closets, lavatories, and drinking fountains that would be required for a nightclub with an occupant load of 600.

Water closets:_____

Lavatories:_____

Drinking fountains:_____

d. How many automatic clothes washers are required in a dormitory with an occupant load of 200?

Explain:_____

_____

_____

e. How many automatic clothes washers are required in an apartment building with 45 dwelling units?_____

_____

f. What are the minimum plumbing fixture requirements for a single-family dwelling?_____

_____

_____

g. For which gender (male or female) are more water closets required in an opera house?

Explain:_____

_____

_____

CHAPTER 8: Electrical and Communication Requirements

PROBLEM 1

Following are different design scenarios. Based on your knowledge of the most current requirements for ground fault circuit interrupters (GFCIs) and arc fault circuit interrupters (AFCIs), as discussed in Chapter 8, answer the questions in the spaces provided.

a. You have been asked to design a kitchen in a condominium unit. Do all the wall receptacle outlets located in this kitchen have to be GFCI-protected?_____

   Why?_____

   _____

   _____

b. If you were designing a restaurant, would all the wall receptacle outlets located in the restaurant kitchen have to be GFCI-protected?_____

   Why?_____

   _____

   _____

c. You have been asked to add a bar sink in the design of the CEO's new executive office. It must also include a receptacle outlet for a coffee maker that will sit on the counter adjacent to the sink. Will this outlet require GFCI protection?_____

   Why?_____

   _____

   _____

d. You are designing the interiors of a new hotel. Instead of table lamps near the beds, wall sconces will be used. Do these wall sconces require AFCI protection?_____

   Why?_____

   _____

   _____

e. You are locating receptacle outlets in the dwelling areas of an assisted living facility. The bathrooms will require a GFCI outlet near the lavatory. Does this bathroom outlet also have to be AFCI-protected?_____

Why?_____

_____

_____

f. In the same assisted living facility, you need to locate receptacle outlets in the employee restroom. This will require an outlet adjacent to the lavatories and another general outlet on the wall across the room. Do both of these require GFCI protection?_____

Why?_____

_____

_____

PROBLEM 2

Refer to *International Energy Conservation Code (IECC)* Table C405.5.2, "Interior Lighting Power Allowances," in Appendix A.15 (or Figure 8.7 in the *Guidebook*) for this problem.

Answer the questions about the following interior lighting scenarios based on your knowledge of energy efficiency and *IECC* Table 505.5.2, including the footnotes. Fill in the answers and explain how you obtained your answers in the spaces provided.

a. You are selecting the light fixtures for a new movie theater. What is the maximum interior lighting power allowance allowed in the building if the total floor area is 41,500 square feet (3855.35 sm)?_____

b. When designing retail spaces, additional lighting power is allowed so that accent lighting can be included to highlight merchandise. Based on footnote "b" in the *IECC* table, what is the lighting power density value for each of the following types of merchandise?

Jewelry:_____

Clothing:_____

Sporting goods:_____

c. You are designing a women's clothing store with a total floor area of 1,800 square feet (167.22 sm). This store sells clothing and jewelry. The clothes sales area consists of 1,100 square feet (102.19 sm) and the jewelry sales area consists of 50 square feet (4.645 sm).

   1. What is the total interior lighting power allowance allowed for general lighting throughout the retail store?_____

   2. What is the additional lighting power allowed specifically to highlight merchandise in the store?_____

d. When selecting light fixtures for a dentist's office with 12-foot (3657.6-mm) ceilings, what is the total interior lighting power allowance allowed in the space if it has a total of 3,100 square feet (287.99 sm)?_____

e. What is the total interior lighting power allowance allowed in a building with the following uses: a car manufacturing facility with a floor area of 83,000 square feet (7710.7 sm) and an adjacent corporate office with a floor area of 7,450 square feet (692.105 sm)?_____

Explain:_____

_____

_____

CHAPTER 9: Finish and Furniture Selection

PROBLEM 1

Following are different design scenarios. Based on your knowledge of the variety of tests for interior finishes and furniture, as discussed in Chapter 9, answer the questions in the spaces provided. (*Note:* "No test" can also be used as an answer.)

a. You have chosen a carpet for the floor of an executive's office in a tenant space. Which standard carpet test must this carpet pass?_____

b. You are planning to install this same carpet on the walls in the corridor. Which additional test must this carpet pass?_____

Why?_____

_____

_____

c. You are planning to hang a large tapestry in the reception area of an advertising agency. It covers more than 30 percent of the wall area. Which test must this wall hanging pass?_____

Why?_____

_____

_____

d. You are replacing the pleated draperies in the executive office of a brokerage firm. They are floor to ceiling and cover a window wall that extends the full width of the office. Which test must the fabric in the new pleated draperies pass?_____

Why?_____

_____

e. You are selecting new seating for a lobby in a hospital that does not have an automatic sprinkler system. There will be 3 sofas and 24 upholstered chairs. Which test must this seating pass?_____

Why?_____

_____

_____

f. You are working with a lawyer who wants to hang a small fabric wall hanging behind the desk in his office. It covers less than 10 percent of the wall. Which test must the wall hanging pass?_____

Why?_____

_____

_____

g. The same client also wants you to select two upholstered guest chairs for his private office. Name two different tests the upholstery on these chairs should pass:

1. _____

2. _____

h. A restaurant owner wants you to specify a fabric to be used in one of the private dining rooms. It will be applied to the ceiling, and it will be tufted. Which test must this fabric pass?_____

Why?_____

_____

_____

i. You are asked to specify a mattress for a private home. Which test must this mattress pass?_____

Why?_____

_____

_____

j. Another client asks you to specify a mattress for a new hotel. Which additional tests must these mattresses pass?_____

Why?_____

_____

_____

k. You intend to use an acoustical stretch fabric system in the conference room of a corporate facility. The codes refer to these systems as "site-fabricated stretch systems." What test must this system pass?_____

PROBLEM 2

Refer to *Life Safety Code (LSC)* Table A.10.2.2, "Interior Finish Classification Limitations," in Appendix A.16 (or Figure 9.13 in the *Guidebook*) for this problem.

The floor plan shown in Figure 9.1 is of the first floor of a five-story hotel. It is an existing building without an automatic sprinkler system. The other four floors are strictly hotel rooms. You have been asked to select all new finishes for this building. Based on *LSC* Table A.10.2.2 and your knowledge of means of egress, determine which finish class(es) are allowed for each room labeled on the floor plan. The rooms are listed here. Write the finish class(es) in the spaces provided. Include wall and ceiling finish class(es) and any listed floor finish class(es). (*Note:* This building may consist of more than one occupancy classification.)

1. Main Lobby:_____

2. Ballroom:_____

3. Offices:_____

4. Corridor:_____

5. Single Room:_____

6. Sui
   te:_____

7. Vestibule:_____

8. Exit Stair:_____

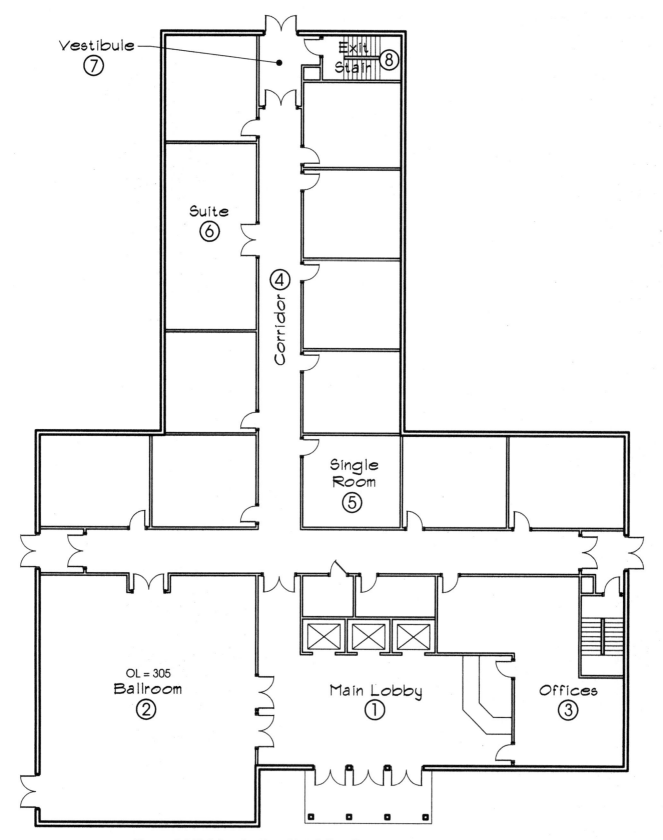

Figure 9.1 Finish selection: Hotel, first floor (nonsprinklered building).

PROBLEM 3

Refer to *LSC* Table A.10.2.2, "Interior Finish Clasification Limitations," in Appendix A.16 (or Figure 9.13 in the *Guidebook*) for this problem.

The following are different scenarios based on the floor plan of the hotel shown in Figure 9.1. Using *LSC* Table A.10.2.2, answer the following questions. Read each scenario carefully and fill in the correct finish class(es) in the spaces provided.

a. You have determined the minimum wall finish required for the Ballroom to be _____. Would there be a difference if an automatic sprinkler system was installed in the entire building?

_____

b. If this were a new, nonsprinklered hotel instead of an existing hotel, which wall and flooring finish classes would be allowed in the Exit Stair?

_____

c. If this new nonsprinklered hotel had a Gift Shop instead of a Ballroom, which two ceiling finish classes would be allowed in the space?

_____

d. If this were an existing, nonsprinklered hospital instead of a hotel, what would be the least strict ceiling finish class allowed in each patient room?

_____

e. If this were an existing, nonsprinklered juvenile detention facility instead of a hotel, which rating would the floor finishes in the exit stair require?

_____

f. If this were a new juvenile detention facility and it had an automatic sprinkler system, what would be the least strict floor finish class allowed in the exit stair?

_____

❏ CHAPTER 10: Code Officials and the Code Process

There are no Study Problems for this chapter.

SECTION 4

ANSWERS TO SHORT-ANSWER QUESTIONS

❏ CHAPTER 1: About the Codes

1. **True.** There are separate federal requirements that these buildings must follow. Typically, each federal agency sets its own requirements. In some cases, an agency may require the use of an ICC or NFPA code; however, their use would then be regulated at a federal level (not a state or local level).

2. **True.** Even if two code jurisdictions require the same code and standard publications, they typically create amendments that slightly modify the code, and they usually have other requirements, such as municipal ordinances, health codes, and zoning regulations, that make their jurisdiction unique.

3. **True.** Many states have chosen to use the *IBC* as a base for their state code. Rather than creating a totally different document, they start with the *International Building Code* and revise certain sections or chapters as needed. In some cases, the code is given a different title but is still published by the ICC.

4. **True.** Most jurisdictions use the NFPA *National Electrical Code (NEC)*. The ICC codes reference it as well.

5. **False.** The *ADA* is not a code. It is a civil rights law that protects against discrimination on the basis of disability. It covers many aspects of disability discrimination, such as employment, communication, transportation, services, and the design of most buildings that are used by the public.

6. **True.** Standards must be referenced by a code publication, be formally adopted by a jurisdiction, or be required by federal law to have legal standing.

7. **True.** Sometimes, stricter requirements are better for the client and/or the safety of the occupants.

8. **False.** Typically, a performance code will apply to only one part or aspect of the project, and prescriptive codes will be used to design the rest of the project.

9. **False.** Only the ICC codes (as well as the last editions of the legacy codes) use the *Common Code Format*. NFPA uses the *Manual of Style*.

10. **False.** Several ICC codes have included provisions regarding indoor air quality for a number of years, including the environmental chapter of the *International Building Code*.

11. *ASHRAE 90.1* (titled the *Energy Standard for Buildings Except Low-Rise Residential Buildings*)

12. occupancy (or occupancy classification)

13. Access Board (or U.S. Access Board or ATBCB)

14. California

15. Underwriters Laboratories (or UL). Another possible answer is NSF International.

16. **c.** Although the NFPA covers these topics in other code documents, such as *NFPA 5000* and *Life Safety Code*, it does not have separate publications for these items.

17. **b.** Although a team approach is recommended, it may not always be required. If it is required, the team leader may vary, but typically he or she must be a licensed design professional. Most often this person will be an architect or an engineer.

18. **a.** The code document you need to reference depends on what is required and/or allowed by the jurisdiction, not the type of the project.

19. **b.** The *ADA* has four title sections. It regulates employment, public accommodations, telecommunications, and transportation. It does not regulate federal buildings or one- and two-family dwellings.

20. **d.**

21. **a.** ANSI approves other organizations to use its ANS consensus process.

22. **d.**

23. **b.** Selecting the strictest (or most restrictive) code requirement will usually work, even if you have to select from a range of dimensions. For example, if the codes require handrails at 30–38 inches (762–965 mm), and the *ADA Standards* allow 34–38 inches (865–965 mm), the ADA is the most restrictive. Using it will satisfy both requirements.

24. **b.** The federal Energy Policy Act (EPAct) mandates that all states adopt the standard *ASHRAE 90.1* (or an acceptable alternate). Each state then mandates requirements at the state and/or local level. (Each jurisdiction also has the option of adopting an energy code such as the ICC's *International Energy Conservation Code*.)

25. **d.** The *NGBS* is a standard, not a code. The *CGBSC* was the first sustainability code.

☐ CHAPTER 2: Occupancy Classifications and Loads

1. **True.** The occupancy classification is needed to determine most of the other code requirements. (It should be determined in conjunction with occupant load.)

2. **False.** The smaller occupancy would be considered an *accessory* occupancy only if it is less than 10 percent of the total area of the two spaces.

3. **False.** Whether the occupant load of a space or building is identified as A-1 (movie theater) versus A-3 (restaurant) or I-2 (hospital) versus I-3 (prison) can have significant effects on which code requirements apply. Occupant load on the other hand is determined by the specific use of the space not the occupancy classification.

4. **True.** If the required fire resistance–rated walls are not properly located in a building with more than one occupancy, the requirements of the most restrictive occupancy will usually apply to all occupancies in the building.

5. **True.** In previous codes, the wall was required to be rated to create a separated occupancy. However, beginning with the 2006 *IBC*, some occupancy classifications with similar risk factors are not required to be separated by a rated wall. (See Table 508.4 in Appendix A.8.)

6. **True.**

7. **False.** The age is the primary determining factor. If the preschoolers are over the age of $2\frac{1}{2}$, then the facility is considered Educational. However, if the preschoolers are $2\frac{1}{2}$ or younger, but there is a door that leads directly to the exterior of the building from the room where they are located, the facility may also be considered Educational. If not, the facility would be considered Institutional.

8. **False.** If bleachers or a designated area for observation is within the pool area, it would be considered an A-4 regardless of the size of the space.

9. **Assembly, Business, Mercantile.** Using the *IBC*, a restaurant could be classified as an Assembly (A-2) or Business (if small). Using the *LSC*, the restaurant could be considered Assembly or Mercantile (if small). For this project, you would have to verify which occupancy classification the local jurisdiction would approve. You would also need to compare the requirements of these two codes and use the most stringent requirements.

10. **Can include:** Detentional/Correctional (or Restrained), Health Care (or Unrestrained), Daycare, or Residential Board and Care

11. risk factors

12. gross

13. physical, health

14. f. Supermarket (Mercantile occupancy)
   g. Refinery (Industrial occupancy)
   b. Gas plant (Hazardous occupancy)
   c. Bank (Business occupancy)
   a. Nursing home (Institutional occupancy)
   h. Kindergarten (Educational occupancy)
   i. Dormitory (Residential occupancy)
   d. Church (Assembly occupancy)
   e. Freight terminal (Storage occupancy)

15. c. Number of occupants is especially important in certain subclassifications of occupancies such as Institutional and Residential (as well as Assembly in the NFPA codes). Unusual hazards and certain types of activities can also change the occupancy classification. The size of the building does not matter, since there may be more than one occupancy classification inside the building. Although the rating of walls is important, they do not determine the occupancy classification. (Note that the building type or use of the space is also required to determine the occupancy classification.)

16. b. Although changing the number of employees can sometimes affect the subclassification of the occupancy, it does not usually affect the main occupancy classification. For example, in a Business occupancy, a fluctuating number of employees will not change the occupancy type. (Note that in Residential and Institutional occupancies, the staff is usually not counted as part of the number of employees.)

17. d. In the *International Building Code*, Assembly subclassifications are based on the type of activity, not the number of occupants. (The NFPA, however, does use the number of occupants to determine the Assembly subclassification.) Educational occupancies are based on the age of the occupant and length of stay.

18. a. A college classroom is usually classified as a Business occupancy. If the classroom is a larger room (e.g., lecture hall type), it may be classified as an Assembly occupancy.

19. c. Although nursing homes can be considered Residential if there is a small number of occupants, they are generally considered an Institutional or Health Care occupancy.

20. a. Depending on the building code, a restaurant is usually considered a Business, Mercantile, or Assembly occupancy. Each of the other building types usually consists of more than one occupancy classification.

21. c. Institutional, Business, and Mercantile occupancies are typically considered public accommodations. Although Factories would be covered by the ADA as commercial facilities, the *ADA Standards* would not apply to this use unless tours of the space were given to the public. Then the path of the tour would have to meet the *ADA Standards*.

22. b. The 10 percent requirement pertains to 10 percent of the entire space (including the accessory use), not just the area of the primary occupancy.

23. d. By definition, mixed multiple occupancies in the NFPA codes and non-separated mixed occupancies in the ICC are not considered separate from each other, so the most stringent requirements will apply.

24. d. Although increasing the occupant load can affect the rating of some walls, such as exit access corridors, it would not require *all* interior walls to be rated.

25. c. The occupant load is typically required to determine means of egress requirements and plumbing fixture quantities. Jurisdictions may also use the occupancy load to determine the maximum number of people allowed to occupy the space at a given time, especially in Assembly occupancies.

26. **a.** Based on the formula, the occupant load is determined by dividing the floor area by the load factor.

27. **d.** The occupant load for each occupancy is determined separately and then added together.

28. **a.** The occupant load is based on the number of people using the space and the load factor provided by the codes. Since these two items can vary based on the building type and use of the space, you may need to do more than one calculation to determine which use will allow the largest number of people.

29. **d.** Fixed seating most often includes benches, bleachers, pews, and booth seating. However, rows of chairs that are rarely moved (i.e., ganged stacking chairs) could also be considered fixed seating.

30. **d.**

☐ CHAPTER 3: Construction Types and Building Sizes

1. **False.** Interior walls do not typically affect the construction type. This can be seen in Figure 3.1 of the *Guidebook*.

2. **True.** In the ICC and NFPA codes, construction types range from Type I, the strictest, to Type V.

3. **True.**

4. **False.** All buildings are classified with a construction type and must maintain the fire resistant ratings of the construction type as defined by the building code at the time it was constructed.

5. **True.**

6. resistant

7. building

8. heavy timber

9. **d.** Some amounts and types of combustible materials are allowed in every construction type. Examples include wood blocking and furring strips. (Also see inset titled *Use of Combustible Materials* in the *Guidebook*.)

10. **b.** Types I and II primarily use noncombustible materials throughout; Type IV consists primarily of heavy timber; and Type V typically uses combustible materials (i.e., wood) for exterior and interior elements.

11. **b.** Chemically treated wood, also known as FRTW, is actually known as *fire retardant*–treated wood.

12. **a.** A fire retardant only delays a combustible material from being consumed by a fire. It will eventually contribute to the fuel of a fire.

13. **c.** A party wall and a fire wall are the same thing. They can be used to create what is considered two or more buildings. A parapet is only the top portion of a fire wall.

14. **a.** Assembly, because of the quantity of occupants; and Institutional, because of the restricted mobility of occupants. (Hazardous occupancies also require stricter construction types.)

15. **d.** The construction type of a building and the use of an automatic sprinkler system can affect the allowable square footage (square meter) or area of a building. However, all three factors must be known to determine if a specific building or space is suitable for a certain use or occupancy type.

16. **d.**

17. **c.** Changing the construction type helps only if it gets stricter. An occupancy separation wall would not help, although a fire wall could make a difference.

18. **b.**

19. **d.**

☐ CHAPTER 4: Means of Egress

1. **False.** A means of egress must be an *unobstructed* path that leads a person safely out of a building. The pathway must meet certain code requirements. For example, although escalators and elevators are often used as part of the general circulation within a building, the codes generally do not allow them to be a means of egress unless very specific code requirements are met (i.e., escalators must be fully enclosed by rated assemblies, and elevator shafts must meet requirements for smoke and fire protection).

2. **False.** In several specific situations, the codes require that the doors within the means of egress swing in the direction of travel. For example, when the occupant load is greater than 49 occupants, or in Hazardous occupancies, the door must swing toward the direction of exit. However, when the occupant load is small, such as in a private office, the door is not usually required to swing toward the exit.

3. **False.** It is the opposite. They must be 10 feet (3048 mm) wide or more to be considered a public way.

4. **True.** There may be some other ways to describe them; however, this is the main difference between the two.

5. **False.** The doorway can be larger than 48 inches (1220 mm) wide. It is the *leaf* of the door that cannot be more than 48 inches (1220 mm) wide.

6. **True.** (Note that the floors below ground level may have different requirements.)

7. Exit access, exit, exit discharge. An area of refuge is another possible answer. An exit discharge can also be an exterior element. A public way is typically an exterior portion of a means of egress.

8. Area of refuge

9. public way. Even if a disabled occupant waits for a time in an area of refuge, the code assumes that the final destination of all occupants is to a public way and out of the building.

10. The most common answers would include: lever, push-type, panic bar, and U-shaped.

11. 12 feet (or 3658 mm)

12. The most common answers would include: no exit, stair number, floor number, and area of refuge.

13. passageway. It is an example of a type of exit discharge.

14. Remotely. The first two exits must follow the half-diagonal rule (or one-third diagonal rule if sprinklered). New editions of the codes emphasize that the loss of one exit should not decrease the exiting capacity by more than half.

15. emergency lighting and luminous egress path markings (required in high-rise buildings only)

16. **b.** An exterior door (exit)
    a. A corridor (exit access)
    a. An office (exit access)
    b. A stairwell (exit)
    c. After descending four flights of stairs, you leave the stairwell and find yourself in the lobby (exit discharge)
    c. An alley that is 8 feet (2438 mm) wide but open to the sky (exit discharge)
    a. An aisle in an open office area between furniture system workstations (exit access)

17. **d.** The allowed fire (and smoke) ratings of walls and other assemblies, as well as allowed finishes, are based on the type of means of egress. Occupant load is used to determine the means of egress.

18. **d.**

19. **a.**

20. **b.** Exits must always be fully enclosed; exit accesses do not. *Exit access stairs* are sometimes allowed to be open when they connect a limited number of floors within the same tenant space. *Intervening rooms* such as reception areas are not always fully enclosed.

21. **a.** 90 inches (2286 mm) is the required ceiling height, but some items are allowed to project down from the ceiling a maximum of 10 inches (254 mm) for a minimum head clearance of 80 inches (2032 mm).

22. **b.** A corridor can be used in a means of egress in three ways. A corridor used as an exit is called an *exit passageway.* A corridor used as an exit access is called an *exit access corridor.* A corridor used as an exit discharge is called a *discharge corridor.*

23. **b.**

24. **a.** The minimum clear opening is 32 inches (813 mm). A 36-inch (914-mm) door is typically required to create 32 inches (813 mm) of clear width.

25. **b.** 7 inches (178 mm) is typically the maximum dimension, not the minimum; spiral stairs are allowed in limited areas and conditions; and the codes allow some exceptions to stairs with handrails on both sides (especially in some Residential occupancies).

26. **a.** This is most typically found in hospitals and prisons. Others would include Storage and Industrial occupancies (and large high-rise buildings).

27. **c.** File/storage rooms are more likely to be locked. They may also contain hazardous contents.

28. **a.** If required, the area of refuge must be located adjacent to the elevator shaft (similar to Plan C in Figure 4.13, as shown in the *Guidebook),* not anywhere on the floor.

29. **d.** A sprinkler system is not required.

30. **b.** You must calculate each tenant or occupant load separately and add them together to determine the number of exits for a whole floor.

31. **c.** 44 inches (1118 mm) is the typical minimum building code corridor width; 36 inches (914 mm) is allowed in some Residential occupancies, and is the typical minimum accessible corridor width.

32. **d.** All are allowed exceptions.

33. **d.**

34. **b.** Longer lengths are usually allowed in buildings equipped with an automatic sprinkler system.

35. **d.** The location of an exit is typically determined by the half-diagonal rule.

36. **b.** The width of an exit in a means of egress should never be reduced as it travels toward the exit discharge.

37. **c.** In determining the required width, the codes require that an additional 19 inches (483 mm), not 18 inches (457 mm), be added to the code minimum or required calculation.

38. **d.** The *International Building Code (IBC)* (or other building code such as the *NFPA 5000* or a locally developed code) and the *Life Safety Code (LSC)* have specific requirements for stairs. When using the *ICC Performance Code (ICCPC),* meeting the criteria and performance codes for the means of egress may also affect the location and configuration of the stair. This would be part of the information reviewed by the code official.

CHAPTER 5: Fire and Smoke Resistant Assemblies

1. **False.** A *passive* fire protection system is what is sometimes referred to as a prevention system.

2. **False.** The fire resistance rating can also be controlled by the walls that surround the floor/ceiling assembly. For example, the codes require certain rooms within a building (such as a mechanical or boiler room) to be surrounded by fire barriers and horizontal assemblies. In addition, floor/ceiling assemblies may be required to be rated in order to separate occupancies on different floors of a building.

3. **False.** Most fire protection rated doors must have a closing device, but it does not necessarily have to be automatic-closing. A self-closing device can also be used. A self-closing device, such as a door closer, will close the door after each use. An automatic-closing device is usually activated by an alarm so that it closes a door that is typically used in the open position.

4. **True.** For example, a rated door can be considered a through-penetration, and typically has a lower rating than the rated wall in which it is located.

5. **False.** The requirements to make a fire-rated door and a smokestop door are different. Smokestop doors are specially designed to inhibit the passage of smoke and must pass additional testing.

6. **False.** It takes vertical fire barriers and horizontal assemblies to create a complete compartmentation.

7. **False.** Although they are similar, occupancy separation walls separate different occupancies within the same building. A demising wall is another name for a tenant separation wall, which separates different tenants of the same occupancy types. Walls that separate different occupancies or tenants are often required to be rated in order to separate the different uses. The term *tenant separation* is rarely used in the more current editions of the codes and most often refers to the separation of tenants in covered malls. These tenants may be of the same occupancy classification.

8. **False.** Most fire protection–rated doors are allowed to have glass lites. However, the codes specify the type of glass that can be used, and sometimes limit the size of the glass.

9. fire (or party)

10. hardware (or sill, or doorway)

11. A smoke barrier. A smoke partition only limits the passage of smoke.

12. a. *Installation of Smoke Door Assemblies and Other Opening Protectives (NFPA 105)*
    e. *Fire Doors and Other Opening Protectives (NFPA 80)*
    f. *Fire Test for Window and Glass Block Assemblies (NFPA 257)*
    b. *Fire Tests of Door Assemblies (NFPA 252)*
    d. *Test of Fire Resistance of Building Construction and Materials (NFPA 251)*
    c. *High-Challenge Fire Walls, Fire Walls, and Fire Barrier Walls (NFPA 221)*

13. c.

14. **a.** Fireblocks and draftstops are used in concealed spaces. A firestop can be constructed in the field as a firestop system, or a prefabricated firestop device can be used.

15. **d.** Common examples include an exit stair that serves more than four stories, a horizontal exit, and an exit passageway.

16. **b.** Fireblocking is used in small, concealed spaces. Firestops and dampers are used at openings in rated assemblies.

17. c.

18. **a.** It can be required in both a separated mixed occupancy, according to the *IBC*, and in a separated multiple occupancy, according to the NFPA codes.

19. **d.** Tempered glass is typically not rated. Only if it is specially treated can it receive a 20-minute rating.

20. **d.** Fully enclosed smoke barriers require additional ventilation and air circulation.

21. **a.** Most fire-rated doors have to be tested by the hose stream test; however, corridors and smoke barriers do not.

22. **d.** All are common examples of fire partitions required by the *IBC*.

23. c.

24. **d.** Smoke barriers prevent the movement of smoke. Pressurized exits prevent smoke from following escaping occupants. Sprinklers concentrate on controlling a fire.

25. **b.** Ceiling dampers are used at a duct or diffuser located in a suspended ceiling to prevent heat from entering the space between the suspended ceiling and the rated floor assembly above.

26. **c.** Smoke dampers are typically used inside the duct.

27. **d.** An electrical box can compromise the rating of a rated wall, but only if it is not installed properly.

28. **d.** Safety wired glass (which is typically a laminated product) could be used; however, traditional wired glass is not allowed in areas where impact is a concern.

29. **a.** The maintenance department is not a reliable source.

❑ CHAPTER 6: Fire Protection Systems

1. **False.** Both multiple- and single-station smoke detectors must be tied into the building's power source.

2. **False.** Although budget may be a consideration, the choice of system will most often be dictated by the codes based on the occupancy type.

3. **False.** New technology (i.e., building automation systems) allows fire and smoke alarm systems to be tied to other building controls such as the mechanical system or the security system, although some jurisdictions may restrict the extent of these connections.

4. **False.** Depending on the type of detector, a detection system can detect smoke and other gases, heat and changes in temperature, or multiple symptoms of fire.

5. **True.** An alarm system can be activated manually using a pull station, or automatically upon the operation of an automatic sprinkler system, fire detection system, or smoke detection system.

6. **True.** (See Figure 6.2 in the *Guidebook*.)

7. **False.** Fire extinguishers can be surface mounted using a bracket, or recessed within a wall using a cabinet. The cabinet can have either a vision panel or a solid door that is clearly marked.

8. visual (visible)

9. 75 feet (or 22,860 mm)

10. **d.** *Portable Fire Extinguishers (NFPA 10)*
    e. *National Fire Alarm Code and Signaling Code (NFPA 72)*
    a. *National Electrical Code (NFPA 70)*
    f. *Installation of Sprinkler Systems (NFPA 13)*
    b. *Emergency and Standby Power Systems (NFPA 110)*
    g. *Fire Safety and Emergency Symbols (NFPA 170)*
    c. *Carbon Dioxide Extinguishing Systems (NFPA 12)*

11. **a.** Emergency voice/alarm communication systems use an intercom to verbally direct the occupants out of a building. Visual/audible alarm systems use a number of different sounds and light patterns to direct occupants, but no verbal direction. An accessible warning system encompasses devices that would be used in addition to typical visual, audio, and voice communication systems (i.e., tactile notification, text messaging, etc.).

12. **d.**

13. **c.** A firestop is a through-penetration protective and part of a prevention system. A manual fire alarm is part of the detection system because it is a device activated by an occupant upon detection of a fire.

14. **c.** Placing a smoke detector too close to the intersection may not provide accurate detection. Codes and standards require a smoke detector to be a minimum of 4 inches (102 mm) from a wall/ceiling intersection so that air currents do not cause smoke and heat to bypass the unit. Heat and smoke detectors are often used together to require two indicators of fire for more accurate detection.

15. b. A manual alarm system is considered a detection system because it is used by an occupant after he or she detects a fire.

16. c. Emergency voice/alarm communication systems are most often required in high-rise buildings, as well as hazardous building types such as factories and large storage facilities.

17. d. Class II is designed specifically for occupant use. Class I is primarily for fire department use. Class III allows for both.

18. b. Although usually located in stairwells, the quantity of stairs does not determine if a standpipe is required.

19. d.

20. b. In a dry pipe system, the pipes are filled with pressurized air or nitrogen until the heat from a fire causes the pipes to fill with water.

21. a. When an automatic sprinkler system is provided in a building, the codes allow a variety of trade-offs, but sprinklers do not affect the occupancy classification of a building or space. (See Figure 6.6 in the *Guidebook* for additional allowances or trade-offs.)

22. b. Sprinkler head types include standard, fast-response, residential, quick-response, extended coverage, open, and large-drop, as well as other specialty types. Sprinkler-head *orientations* include pendant, upright, sidewall, recessed, and concealed.

23. b. This is typical, although specialty sprinklers may require additional clearances.

24. d. Accessibility requirements cover alarm and accessible warning systems, as well as a few general requirements such as reaching distances and protrusions into the path of travel.

25. a. The codes often limit the use of sprinklers in restaurant kitchens due to the amount of heat that is naturally created and the possibility of grease fires. Non-water-based extinguishing systems are typically used instead. However, sprinklers are usually required in kitchen exhaust systems.

26. a. (See Figure 6.5 in the *Guidebook*.)

❏ CHAPTER 7: Plumbing and Mechanical Requirements

1. True. This is especially true of the I-Codes, since the *IBC* includes the table for plumbing fixtures as well as other facility requirements. The building codes also typically include requirements for plumbing-related items such as standpipes, fire hoses, and sprinkler systems.

2. False. Generally, every floor will require a minimum of one toilet or restroom per gender—one male and one female. In some cases, these can be combined into a single unisex toilet facility when the occupant load is limited.

3. False. It is the other way around. There are usually more water closets than lavatories.

4. False. Particularly with the increase in use of automatic fixtures, coordination between plumbing and electrical is equally important. Along with the mechanical needs, plumbing, electrical, and mechanical requirements can affect a number of other building elements, such as the height of a suspended ceiling.

5. True. Both documents include water consumption requirements. The energy code requirements are typically more stringent.

6. False. Not only are some of the requirements found in the building codes (including the environmental chapters) and the energy codes, but there are also a number of standards, such as those from ASHRAE.

7. True.

8. contractor

9. nonabsorbent

10. water closet

11. $6\frac{1}{2}$ inches (165 mm)

12. ventilation

13. load

14. d. In addition to all plumbing fixtures, sprinklers, standpipes, fire hoses, and fire extinguishers are also part of a building's plumbing system.

15. a. You need to determine the occupancy classification of a project before you can determine the occupant load. The occupant load is then used with the code tables to determine the quantity and type of fixtures.

16. b. The *IPC* now requires the total occupant load to be divided in half before doing any calculations using the *IPC* table. When calculating a building or floor with more than one occupancy, each should be calculated separately and then added together before any rounding is done.

17. c. A toilet in a tenant space cannot be deducted from the total common facilities required for that floor, since it is not available for everyone on the floor to use.

18. d. In the past codes and ADA requirements, if a single urinal was required, it had to be accessible. However, since an accessible toilet has to be provided along with a urinal, the accessible toilet satisfies the accessibility requirement.

19. a. A unisex toilet may be required when six or more water closets are provided, not eight. A required unisex (or family/assisted-use) toilet facility is typically counted in the total number of plumbing fixtures.

20. d. The plumbing codes specify the finish requirements of a plumbing fixture.

21. b. Some accessibility documents may allow between 16 and 18 inches (405 and 455 mm), but 18 inches (455 mm) is most common; 15 inches (381 mm) is what is required by codes for nonaccessible water closets.

22. a. They are most commonly used in schools, restaurants, clubs, lounges, transportation terminals, auditoriums, theaters, and churches. All of these can be classified as an Assembly or an Educational occupancy.

23. d. Drinking fountains located in corridors often violate the 4-inch (100 mm) protrusion limit in the ADA requirements, *ICC A117.1*, and other accessibility guidelines. This is why drinking fountains are often located in recesses.

24. b.

25. c. The codes require water closets to have an elongated bowl with a seat open at the front. Bathtubs are typically required only in Residential occupancies. The swing of a door will affect the length and/or depth of an accessible toilet stall. Accessible sinks and lavatories have similar kneespace and toespace requirements.

26. b. A drinking fountain can be installed in the corridor leading to a toilet facility, but the codes do not allow one in the vestibule leading into the toilet facility. Laminate is considered impervious material and therefore can be used on toilet stalls. There is no problem with mounting all toilet accessories at the same accessible height, even though only a percentage are required to be accessible.

27. d. Although water closets and bathing fixtures require a variety of clear floor space sizes, 30 by 48 inches (760 by 1220 mm) is required at almost all other accessible plumbing fixtures and accessories.

28. d. Residential occupancies include dormitories, hotels, and apartments. Assembly occupancies include gymnasiums and health clubs. Institutional occupancies include hospitals, prisons, and nursing homes. (Although dormitories and gymnasiums may be located in an educational facility, they are often considered a separate occupancy. Only certain Industrial occupancies require shower facilities.)

29. **c.** The height of the walls surrounding a shower must be a minimum of 70 inches (1778 mm) above the shower drain. A curb at an accessible shower can be as high as 0.5 inch (13 mm). However, if it is more than 0.25 inch (6.4 mm) high, the edges must be beveled. Certain roll-in shower configurations allow an accessible lavatory within the clear floor space of the shower.

30. **d.** It is appropriate to use the symbol in all these locations. A building with a nonaccessible toilet facility must include the symbol on the sign to indicate the location to the nearest accessible facility. (In new buildings it is common not to show the symbol on any of the toilet facilities because all of them should be accessible.)

31. **b.** Suspended ceilings create a horizontal ceiling plenum. It is the plenum that is used to return the air; ducts are only used to supply the conditioned air. A shaft plenum would be vertical.

32. **d.**

33. **c.** The office would most likely be grouped together with the other interior offices into one zone. (If it were a larger executive office, it might be given its own thermostat.)

34. **a.** Ducts are still needed in plenum air systems, but only to supply the air to the space. The codes prohibit the use of combustible materials in a plenum space.

35. **d.** The type of lavatory faucet will determine the water flow rate. An energy-efficient thermostat typically has to be programmable. Window treatments can affect the cooling load of a building.

☐ CHAPTER 8: Electrical and Communication Requirements

1. **True.** (The ICC stopped publishing the *ICC Electrical Code—Administrative Provisions (ICCEC)* in 2006, which referenced the *NEC* as well.)

2. **True.**

3. **False.** They are also installed in ceilings for light fixtures.

4. **False.** They are similar, but not the same. Both are used to supply power when the normal power source fails. However, an *emergency power system* is for operating emergency systems, such as exit signs, emergency lighting, and automatic door locks; a *standby power system* is used for less critical building systems, such as mechanical systems, general lighting, and elevators.

5. **False.** In the most recent codes, AFCI requirements apply to all electrical outlets, including wall, floor, and ceiling outlets, as well as light fixtures and smoke detectors in most living areas of a dwelling unit, not just sleeping rooms.

6. **True.**

7. ground

8. 6 feet (1.8 meters). This is typically accomplished by placing an outlet every 12 feet (3656 mm) along a wall. (Note that in commercial applications, receptacles are typically placed for convenience.)

9. ten (10)

10. wattage

11. voltage(s)

12. **b.** *NFPA 70* is the same thing as the *National Electrical Code.*

13. **a.** The designer will typically locate the outlets and determine the type of light fixtures. The engineer will design the corresponding electrical system and confirm that everything meets the electrical codes.

14. **d.**

15. a. Typically, an electrical panel is considered a panelboard or switchboard by the level of power being managed and if the panel is one or two sided. The service entrance can be a switchboard or a panelboard. Once in the building and distributed to a secondary switchboard or panelboard, the branch panelboards supply electricity to different areas on the same floor.

16. d.

17. a. Flex cable is the same thing as BX cable, which is often used on suspended light fixtures.

18. c. It is typically prohibited in residential, hospital, and school buildings. The *NEC* also prohibits the use of flat wire in wet and other hazardous areas.

19. a. Romex cables are typically limited to one- and two-family dwellings and multi-unit dwellings.

20. a. Conduit is also available in plastic, but is typically allowed only in nonrated applications.

21. d. A smokestop would be required if it was a smoke barrier. A fire damper is used when ductwork passes through a fire barrier.

22. c. This code requirement applies to electrical boxes, as well as wires, cables, and conduit.

23. b. A junction box is a generic electrical box where wires can be terminated for future use, spliced together to add additional devices, and so on. It allows access to these wires.

24. b. This is the lowest reaching height allowed for a person in a wheelchair.

25. a. Even though only UL-approved (or labeled) light fixtures can be used on the interior of a building, the light fixture must be specially rated to be allowed in fire resistance-rated ceilings.

26. d. In dwelling units, typically only the outlets located near cabinetry or the wet area must be GFCI. This applies to individual sinks in other occupancies as well. However, in commercial restrooms and commercial/institutional kitchens, typically all outlets in the room must be GFCI.

27. b. Hanging (or pendant) light fixtures are allowed, but they must be mounted so that they are located outside the restricted area around the tub or shower. (See Figure 8.6 in the *Guidebook*.) Wall sconces that are deeper than 4 inches (100 mm) must be mounted more than 80 inches (2032 mm) above the floor.

28. b. Artificial lighting must be present in exit discharges only when the building is in use.

29. d.

30. d.

31. a.

32. c. Although in the past, a communication system consisted primarily of a telephone system, it now can include computer data, intercom, security, cable, and satellite services, as well as the many options now available with alarm systems.

33. c. Similar to electrical closets, communication and satellite rooms usually do not have to meet requirements as stringent as the main communication room.

34. e. Fiber-optic cable (provides the highest speed and capacity)
  d. Twisted-pair cable (are rated by category)
  b. Wireless (uses transmitters to connect users to system)
  f. Zone cabling (uses intermediate terminals in ceilings)
  g. Circuit integrity cable (provides a 2-hour fire rating)
  a. Coaxial cable (commonly used for video transmissions)
  c. Composite cable (bundles various types of cables into one sleeve)

35. c. Cable trays are not the only method to neatly run cables in a ceiling. Only abandoned cables that are accessible (i.e., easily reached) must be removed. Although electrical and communication outlets are usually mounted adjacent to each other, the cables are not typically allowed to share the same conduit.

1. **True.**

2. **True.**

3. **False.** To pass the *CAL 133* test, a piece of furniture must be tested as a whole. That means setting the sofa on fire, which would ruin it.

4. **True.** If wood veneer is used as a wallcovering, for example, it may have to meet the requirements of the *Steiner Tunnel Test* or the *Room Corner Test*. An intumescent paint or coating may be used to improve its rating.

5. **False.** The thermally thin requirement in the codes is limited to finishes applied to *noncombustible* surfaces, such as gypsum board, plaster, brick, or concrete.

6. **True.** Required finish classes become stricter as you move from an interior room to an exit access corridor or an exit stair, so that as the occupants move away from the flames, the way to safety is free of fire and smoke.

7. **False.** If a finish is not tested, it may be possible to treat it to obtain the appropriate rating.

8. **False.** It is the other way around. Typically a product certification program will use one of the standards as a benchmark within the certification process.

9. block (or blocker)

10. Flashover

11. treatment

12. worksurfaces (or tables or desks or counters)

13. organic

14. **b.** *Pill Test (16 CFR 1630)*
    h. *Steiner Tunnel Test (ASTM E84)*
    e. *Vertical Flame Test (NFPA 701)*
    c. *Radiant Panel Test (ASTM E648)*
    a. *Room Corner Test (NFPA 265)*
    f. *Toxicity Test (NFPA 269)*
    d. *Smolder Resistance Test (NFPA 260)*
    g. *Mattress Test (16 CFR 1632)*

15. **b.** (See Figure 9.3 in the *Guidebook.*)

16. **c.** This test is required in building types such as hospitals and jails, as well as Residential occupancies such as hotels and dormitories. (*16 CFR 1632* is also a mattress test, but is required by the federal government on all mattresses sold in the United States.)

17. **c.** Also known as the *Flooring Radiant Panel Test*, it is primarily used for rating interior floor finishes.

18. **d.** The *Pitts Test* is a toxicity test, which is used to test a wide variety of finishes, furnishings, and building materials.

19. **a.** Although certain occupancies may typically have different building sizes than others, it is the occupancy classification, not the building size, that matters. The location of a finish, especially in a means of egress, makes a difference as well. The jurisdiction also affects what is required, both by mandating a specific code publication and by amending the code to require additional finish and furniture standards.

20. **b.** The test results in a pass/fail, not a class rating. The *Life Safety Code* (starting with the 2003 edition) now references the ASTM version, and the *International Fire Code* (starting with the 2009 edition) now references both versions. The tests are not referenced in the *International Building Code*.

21. **d.** (See Figure 9.3 in *Guidebook*.)

22. d.

23. a. The *Room Corner Test* is specifically used when napped, tufted, or looped textiles or carpets are used on walls and ceilings.

24. a.

25. b. The *Steiner Tunnel Test* measures the "flame spread" (or FSI) and "smoke development" (or SDI).

26. a. The rating of the wall base should be at least a Class II of the *Radiant Panel Test*, or Class I where Class I flooring is required.

27. c. These types of finishes include draperies and wall hangings, among other things.

28. d. Some fabrics may bleed, shrink, or flatten when a treatment is added. Often, the treatment company will be able to tell from the content of the fabric how it will react to a treatment; however, having a fabric sample tested is the only way to know for sure.

29. d. These include occupancies that have evacuation restrictions and overnight provisions. Building types such as hospitals, prisons, and hotels tend to be the most stringent.

30. a. In buildings that require rated finishes and furniture, the addition of an automatic sprinkler system will often allow finishes with lower ratings to be used. Rarely will the use of sprinklers eliminate the need for rated finishes.

31. c. If any of the listed finishes or materials cover a larger area of a wall area or ceiling than allowed in the code (usually expressed in a percentage of the overall surface area), they are usually required to have a higher finish rating. Furring strips and heavy timber have their own separate requirements.

32. a. Exits typically require higher finish ratings than exit accesses and other interior spaces.

33. b. (See Figure 9.18 in the *Guidebook*.)

34. d. There cannot be a drastic level change between two different types of flooring. Marble floors tend to be thicker than carpet. The marble subfloor typically has to be recessed so that the top of the marble and the carpet will align. Although a carpet pad can create a problem for wheelchair use, thin double-stick pads usually do not.

35. b. Although the test samples in *Smolder Resistance Tests* may include fabrics and foams, the tests were developed specifically for a full mock-up of a piece of furniture rather than individual items.

36. b. The symbols are used primarily on textiles; they are not used on furniture.

37. a. You should keep abreast of the newest finish and furniture code requirements and most advanced industry standards used throughout the country (and in other countries), not just within the jurisdiction of the project. When allowed by the jurisdiction, you may want to use more restrictive finish standards to provide additional safety. Keep a record of your research and why you used certain standards over others. (Also note when a federal requirement is more stringent than a local requirement.)

38. d.

☐ CHAPTER 10: Code Officials and the Code Process

1. False. Projects that require minimal finish and furniture installation will typically not require a permit. Other smaller interior projects, in smaller buildings or residential houses, may not require a permit either, depending on the jurisdiction of the project.

2. True. Because codes typically indicate the final result that must be obtained, there is often more than one way to accomplish that result.

3. False. The board cannot waive a code requirement. It can only decide if the appeal meets the interpretation or intent of the code.

4. **False.** Although some federal agencies do have formal reviews available, this is a lengthy process and should be reserved for very large or public projects. Rather, you should be familiar enough with federal requirements to include the necessary information in your drawings.

5. **True.** Although not always the case, many jurisdictions require the use of LEED, Green Globes, or a residential-type green rating program for certain building types and sizes. (See Appendix B in the *Guidebook* for more information.)

6. department, official

7. permit

8. programming. Although code research will continue throughout the design phases, you should start as soon as possible.

9. contractor (or subcontractor)

10. specifications, schedules and legends. This information is typically included in the project manual (written information about the project) or in the drawing set.

11. **a.** The drawings are reviewed by the plans examiner for code and standards compliance and by the fire marshal for fire code compliance. (In some jurisdictions, this may be one and the same person.) The building inspector checks for compliance in the field during construction.

12. **b.** The correct code jurisdiction must be determined before you know which codes department to contact to answer the remaining questions.

13. **b.** Obtaining a permit is typically done by a contractor or subcontractor.

14. **d.** Permits are typically required when construction or alterations are made to a building, when there is a change in occupancy, and/or when regulated equipment is installed. Projects that require only finish and furniture installation will typically not have to pull a permit. There are some exceptions for large finish installations.

15. c. During the schematic phase, you will have enough drawings done to have them reviewed; if changes must be made, it is less costly to do them at this point rather than in the construction drawing phase.

16. **d.** Cost alone should not be the reason to go through the appeals process. However, if the related cost is disproportionate to the overall cost of the project and a viable alternate solution is available, it is more likely that an appeal will be granted.

17. c. An appeal (or variance) can be used only on the project in question, and all projects requiring a permit must go through the permit review process.

18. **a.** Not all jurisdictions with green rating programs require the use of a green rating system; you need to confirm which program should be used. You may want to hire a third party to assist with the design and documentation of the projects; however, inspections are handled by the codes department and they will determine who does them.

19. **b.** A footing inspection is typically required only in new construction, as this is part of the foundation of a building.

20. **d.** Although the inspector's main job is to make sure the construction meets code, he or she also checks the construction drawings to make sure that what was approved during plan review is being done. The codes department issues a Certificate of Occupancy after the final inspection.

21. **a.** The use of performance codes may allow you more design options, but should not be used strictly for cost savings.

22. **b.** A code department is not required to have the documentation reviewed by an outside consultant. It will depend on the extent of the project, the type of performance criteria used, the format of the documentation, and the expertise of the code official(s).

23. **d.**

24. **b.** Always ask the code official located in the jurisdiction of the project.

SECTION 5

ANSWERS TO STUDY PROBLEMS

❏ CHAPTER 1: About the Codes

PROBLEM 1

Code Organizations:
1. International Code Council (ICC)
2. National Fire Protection Association (NFPA)

Standards Organizations: Possible answers include:
1. American National Standards Institute (ANSI)
2. National Fire Protection Association (NFPA)
3. International Code Council (ICC)
4. ASTM International (or American Society for Testing and Materials)
5. NSF International (or National Sanitation Foundation)
6. American Society of Heating, Refrigeration, and Air-Conditioning Engineers (ASHRAE)
7. Underwriters Laboratories (UL)

Federal Agencies: Possible answers include:
1. Architectural and Transportation Barriers Compliance Board (ATBCB or Access Board)
2. Department of Housing and Urban Development (HUD)
3. Department of Justice (DOJ)
4. Department of Transportation (DOT)
5. Department of Energy (DOE)
6. Department of Defense (DOD)
7. U.S. Postal Service (USPS)

PROBLEM 2

ABA—Architectural Barriers Act
ADA—Americans with Disabilities Act
EPAct—Energy Policy Act
FHA—Fair Housing Act
IBC—*International Building Code*
ICC A117.1— *Standard on Accessible and Useable Buildings and Facilities*
ICCPC—*International Code Council Performance Code*
IEBC—*International Existing Building Code*
IECC—*International Energy Conservation Code*
IFC—*International Fire Code*
IGCC—*International Green Construction Code*
IMC—*International Mechanical Code*
IPC—*International Plumbing Code*
IRC—*International Residential Code*
LSC—*Life Safety Code (or NFPA 101)*
NEC—*National Electrical Code (or NFPA 70)*
NFPA 1—*Fire Code*
UMC—*Uniform Mechanical Code*
UPC—*Uniform Plumbing Code*

CHAPTER 2: Occupancy Classifications and Loads

PROBLEM 1

a. Institutional, Restrained (or I-3).

   Explanation: Prisons are considered Institutional (I) occupancies. Of the four subclassifications listed, I-3 best describes a prison.

b. *IBC*: Residential (or R-1).

   LSC: Hotels and Dormitories.

   Explanation: According to the *IBC*, a hotel would be a Residential occupancy (R-1 specifically). And although hotels are considered a type of residential occupancy in the NFPA codes, they have a specific subclassification for hotels. So, when using the *LSC*, you would refer to the requirements for a Hotels and Dormitories occupancy classification.

c. The expected number of occupants (i.e., employees and patrons).

   Explanation: Although a nightclub is clearly an Assembly (A) occupancy, the NFPA codes further subdivide Assembly occupancies based on the occupant load. Thus, you need to know whether the occupant load will be 50–300, 301–1000, or over 1000. Each subclassification may have different requirements for finishes.

d. Institutional (or I-1), because of the number of residents.

   Explanation: The *IBC* uses the number of residents to determine when an assisted living facility is considered an Institutional (I) occupancy. When more than 16 occupants (not including staff) reside at the facility, it is considered Institutional. If fewer than 16 occupants (not including staff) are at a facility, it could be considered Residential (R-4).

e. Residential—Board and Care, because it is the only appropriate classification according to the *LSC* (or NFPA codes).

   Explanation: The NFPA codes define this type of use in a classification of its own, and it is not separated by number of residents.

PROBLEM 2

Occupant load of Figure 2.1 = 52.

Explanation: The occupant load is determined by calculating the square footage (or square meters) of the space and dividing it by the occupant load factors found in *IBC* Table 1004.1.2. You were told the space is a retail store. This is a Mercantile (M) occupancy. Looking on the table under "Function of Space," there are three categories under "Mercantile." Because you were told that this store is on the ground floor, you will use the second category, "Basement and grade floor areas." This allows you 30 gross square feet (2.8 sm) of area per occupant. Notice, however, that there is also a category called "Storage, stock, shipping areas." If you look at the floor plan, it shows that the rear of the store will be used for storage. This area will be calculated separately using 300 gross square feet (28 sm) per occupant. (Both categories require gross area, so include all miscellaneous spaces in your calculations.)

Because there are two different load factors, two square footage calculations must be made. Using the formula *Occupant Load = Floor Area / Load Factor,* the occupant load is determined as follows:

SPACE	LOAD FACTOR	SIZE OF SPACE	FLOOR AREA	OCCUPANT LOAD
Retail area	30 gross (2.787 sm)	48.5 × 31 (14.78 × 9.45)	1503.5 sf (139.7 sm)	1503.5/30 = 50.12 (139.7/2.787 = 50.12)
Storage area	300 gross (27.87 sm)	14 × 31 (4.27 × 9.45)	434 sf (40.35 sm)	434/300 = 1.45 (40.35/27.87 = 1.45)

Using the calculations for feet and inches, the total occupant load is 50.12 for the retail area, plus 1.45 for the storage area. This equals 51.57, which rounds up to 52. (The codes indicate that you should always round up when a total results in a fraction.)

PROBLEM 3

a. Plan B; because the Storage (S) occupancy is less than 10 percent of the entire building.

Explanation: The storage area in Plan A is small enough to be considered a room within the larger Educational (E) use, but not a separate use.

The storage area in Plan C could not be considered an accessory use either. To be considered an accessory use by the codes, the storage area must be less than 10 percent of the total area. If you add the two spaces together, the total area of the building is 6000 square feet (557.4 sm). To be considered an accessory use, the storage area would have to be less than 10 percent of 6000 square feet (557.4 sm) or 600 square feet (55.7 square feet). Because the area of the Storage (S-1) in Plan C exceeds 10 percent of the total area of the building, it cannot be considered an accessory use to the main Assembly (A-2) occupancy. (Instead, it would be considered a separate occupancy classification from the A-2 and the building would be considered a mixed occupancy.)

In the case of Plan D, the Storage (S-1) use is larger than the Factory (F) use and thus cannot be considered an accessory use. (This would also be considered a mixed-occupancy building.)

b. Occupant load of Figure 2.2 Plan A = 250.

Explanation: The occupant load is determined by calculating the square feet (or square meters) of the space and dividing it by the occupant load factors found in *IBC* Table 1004.1.2 for each type of use. To determine the occupant load for the entire building, you must first calculate the occupant load of each occupancy type or use and then add them together. First, start by calculating the occupant load of the Educational (E) area. To do this, you divide the area of the Educational portion of the building by the load factor found in the *IBC* table. The area of the Educational part of the building is shown on Plan A to be 5000 square feet (464.5 sm). In Table 1004.1.2, you can see that the Educational use has two separate load factors. You were told that the Educational use was primarily classrooms, so you will use the load factor given for "Classroom area," which is 20 net square feet (1.858 sm) per occupant.

Occupant Load = Floor Area/Load Factor

Occupant Load = 5000 NSF/20 NSF = 250 occupants

or:

Occupant Load = 464.5 NSM/1.858 NSM = 250 occupants

Now consider the area of the Storage use. Because the Storage area was determined in the previous question not to be a separate use, it is considered to be a part of the Educational use. Notice that the load factor used to determine the occupant load of the Educational area requires a net area. For uses that require net areas to be used, utility or nonoccupied spaces are not included. Thus, the area of the Storage room is not used to calculate the total occupant load of the building. The total occupant load for the building remains at 250 occupants.

PROBLEM 4

a. Occupant load of the entire building in Figure 2.3 = 241.

Explanation: To determine the occupant load of the entire building, you add all the occupant loads (OL) given. The Meeting Room (A-2) includes two separate occupant loads because this space is used in two different ways. Sometimes it is used with tables and chairs (for example, for a luncheon) and sometimes it is used with only chairs (for example, for a lecture). These different uses would result in different occupant loads. You must use the occupant load that results in the highest concentration of people, which is 171. Add this to the other occupant loads provided: 171 + 35 + 20 +15 = 241.

b. Occupant load that is required to accommodate the Central Hall in Figure 2.3 = 139.

Explanation: This situation is an example of having to combine the occupant loads of primary and secondary spaces in order to determine the total occupant load. So, to determine the occupant load of the Central Hall area, you must first determine the occupant load for that specific space and then add the number of occupants from the adjacent areas that must pass through the Central Hall on their way to the final exit.

First, you are given the occupant load for the Central Hall for its specific use. The area that is used by tables and chairs has an occupant load of 20. The other area of the Central Hall is assumed to be pathways for the egress of the other areas. Also, because the majority of the adjacent spaces are Assembly uses, the additional area in the Central Hall can be considered part of the egress and would not be required to be figured as additional occupant load.

Now, you must consider the adjacent spaces. First, look at the Meeting Room (A-2). As you can see on the floor plan, one of the exits from the Meeting Room empties into the Central Hall. Since there are two exits, you can assume that half of the 171 occupants, or 86 occupants, would exit into the Central Hall from the Meeting Room. Thus, the number of occupants that the Meeting Room will contribute to the Central Hall is 86.

Next you must consider the Library (A-3). One of the two exits empties into the Central Hall. You are told that the occupant load of the Library is 35. Again, you can assume that half of the occupants will exit from each exit; so, rounding up, the number of occupants that the Library will contribute to the Central Hall is 18.

The Administrative Offices (B) have no direct exits to the exterior. In this case, all of the 15 occupants from this area must exit into the Central Hall to reach an exit., Therefore, the number of occupants that the Administrative Offices will contribute to the Central Hall is 15.

To calculate the final occupant load for the Central Hall, you now add the occupant loads of each of the areas together:

$$20 + 86 + 18 + 15 = 139$$

The total occupant load that must be accommodated from the Central Hall is 139. (*Note*: In calculating the occupant loads, no occupants are attributed to the toilet facilities because those occupants are already included in the occupant loads for the other areas.)

c. No. The number of exits provided in the layout for the spaces is sufficient or exceed the required number of exits, except for the Central Hall space.

Explanation: The Meeting Room has an occupant load of more than 49 occupants, which according to the code is the point at which two exits from a space are required. Two exits are provided. Although the Library only has an occupant load of 35 and requires only one exit, two are provided. The Administrative Offices have an occupant load of 15, so only one exit from the space is required and only one is provided. However, based on the calculations from the previous question, 139 occupants must be accommodated from the Central Hall. There is only one exit currently indicated from this space. (Two doors are shown in the same location but that is only considered one exit). This design would have to be reworked to provide an additional exit in the Central Hall to accommodate the occupant load of 139.

PROBLEM 5

a. Occupant load of Figure 2.4 = 144.

Explanation: A church is considered an Assembly (A-3) occupancy. You are told that this church has permanent continuous pews, so you would look on *IBC* Table 1004.1.2 under "Assembly with fixed

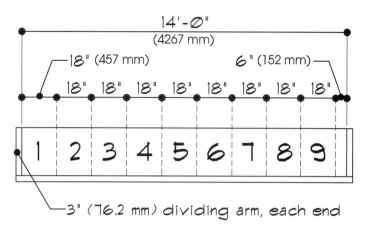

Figure 2.4a. Continuous Pews (Answer).

seats." However, instead of giving you a square footage factor, this refers you to another section of the code. From what you have learned about determining the occupant load with fixed seats, you know that this section of the code indicates that the occupant load for fixed seats is typically determined by counting the fixed seats. However, since the pews do not have dividing arms, the capacity of the seats is based on one person for every 18 inches (457 mm) of seating length, as explained in the *Guidebook*.

You are told that each pew is 14'-6" (4419.6 mm) long. However, this dimension includes the 3-inch (76.2 mm) thick arms at each end. The actual sitting length is 14 feet, or 168 inches (14 × 12 inches), or 4267 mm. To determine how many persons are allowed on one pew, divide 168 by the 18 inches (4267 by 457 mm) per person. You get 9.3 people. But a fraction of a person cannot sit down, so you must round down to 9 persons per pew. (This is illustrated by the drawing in Figure 2.4a.)

The church floor plan shows that there are 16 equal-size pews. To get the total occupant load for the church, multiply these 16 pews by 9, to get 144.

b. Occupant load of Figure 2.4 with dividing arms = 128.

Explanation: Instead of having continuous pews like the first part of this problem, the row is now divided into individual seats by dividing arms. Therefore, instead of dividing the length of the row by 18 inches, the codes tell you to count the actual seats. Figure 2.5 shows that there are 8 seats per pew. Multiply this by the 16 pews shown in the floor plan and you get an occupant load for the space of 128 (8 × 16 = 128).

PROBLEM 6

a. No, because the total area of the building is 9200 square feet (854.7 sm) and based on the occupant load calculations, it will only allow 46 occupants. (The developer wants to accommodate 54 occupants).

Explanation: To check the developer's assumption of occupant load appropriate for the building, you need to determine the allowable occupant load for the area of the building or determine the area that would be needed for the desired occupant load.

First, an apartment complex is considered a Residential (R) occupancy. Using the known area of the building and the load factor from the table for Residential, you can determine how many occupants are allowed in the 9200-square-foot (854.7-sm) building:

Occupant Load = Floor Area/Load Factor

Occupant Load = 9200 GSF/200 GSF = 46 occupants

or:

Occupant Load = 854.7 GSM/18.58 GSM = 46 occupants

This indicates that the area of the existing building will only accommodate 46 occupants. (The developer had assumed 54.)

Alternate Explanation: Now, using the occupant load formula, determine the required floor area:

$$\text{Occupant Load} = \text{Floor Area}/\text{Load Factor}$$

$$\text{Floor Area} = \text{Load Factor} \times \text{Occupant Load}$$

$$\text{Floor Area} = 200\ \text{GSF} \times 54\ \text{occupants} = 10{,}800\ \text{gross square feet}$$

or:

$$\text{Floor Area} = 18.58\ \text{GSM} \times 54\ \text{occupants} = 1003.3\ \text{gross square meters}$$

This indicates that the necessary area required by the codes for 54 occupants is larger than the actual area of the building.

b. Yes, because the 8400 square feet (780.4 sm) required for a retirement center with this many occupants is within the 9200 square feet (854.7 sm) of the building (*or* because a 9200-square-foot [854.7-sm] building allows 75 occupants for a retirement center but the developer wants to accommodate only 70 occupants).

Explanation: Use the occupant load formula to find the floor area required for a retirement center with this many occupants. The occupant load is the total expected number of occupants, including tenants and employees: 62 + 8 = 70 occupants. The load factor of 120 gross square feet (11.148 sm) is found in *IBC* Table 1004.1.2 under "Institutional occupancy" with the subheading of "Sleeping areas." (*Note:* Health services are provided, so this is considered an Institutional occupancy, not a Residential occupancy.) Plug these figures into the formula to determine how many square feet (or square meters) are required.

$$\text{Occupant Load} = \text{Floor Area}/\text{Load Factor}$$

$$\text{Floor Area} = \text{Load Factor} \times \text{Occupant Load}$$

$$\text{Floor Area} = 120\ \text{GSF} \times 70\ \text{occupants} = 8400\ \text{gross square feet}$$

or:

$$\text{Floor Area} = 11.148\ \text{GSM} \times 70\ \text{occupants} = 780.4\ \text{gross square meters}$$

This indicates that the floor area necessary for the desired occupant load is within the area of the existing building.

Alternate Explanation: You can also use the same formula and load factor to determine the maximum number of occupants allowed in a 9200-square-foot (854.7-sm) building:

$$\text{Occupant Load} = \text{Floor Area}/\text{Load Factor}$$

$$\text{Occupant Load} = 9200\ \text{GSF}/120\ \text{GSF} = 76.6 = 77\ \text{occupants}$$

or:

$$\text{Occupant Load} = 854.7\ \text{GSM}/11.148\ \text{GSM} = 76.6,\ \text{or } 77\ \text{occupants}$$

This indicates that the area of the building will allow more occupants than necessary.

c. No, because even though the first floor falls within the area requirements, the second floor does not (*or* because the expected occupant load for the second floor is higher than that allowed by the codes).

Explanation: A retail center falls under the Mercantile (M) occupancy on *IBC* Table 1004.1.2. However, Mercantile is further divided into "Basement and grade floor areas," with a load factor of 30 gross square feet (2.79 sm), and "Areas on other floors," with a load factor of 60 gross square feet (5.574 sm). Both apply to the proposed retail center. Use these load factors and the expected number of occupants to determine the required area (square feet or square meters) for each floor:

First Floor:

$$\text{Occupant Load} = \text{Floor Area}/\text{Load Factor}$$

$$\text{Floor Area} = \text{Load Factor} \times \text{Occupant Load}$$

Floor Area = 30 GSF × 125 occupants = 3750 gross square feet

or:

Floor Area = 2.79 GSM × 125 occupants = 348.8 gross square meters

Second Floor:

Occupant Load = Floor Area / Load Factor

Floor Area = Load Factor × Occupant Load

Floor Area = 60 GSF × 85 occupants = 5100 gross square feet

or:

Floor Area = 5.574 GSM / 85 occupants = 473.8 gross square meters

Each floor in the building has 4600 square feet (427.3 sm). The first-floor calculation falls within this, at 3750 square feet (348.8 sm). The calculation for the second floor requires 5100 square feet (473.8 sm), which is too high for the actual space.

Alternate Explanation: You can also use the same formula and load factors to determine the maximum number of occupants allowed on each of the 4600-square-foot (427.3-sm) floors:

First Floor:

Occupant Load = Floor Area / Load Factor

Occupant Load = 4600 GSF / 30 GSF = 153.3 = 154 occupants

or:

Occupant Load = 427.3 GSM / 2.79 GSM = 153.2 = 154 occupants

Second Floor:

Occupant Load = Floor Area / Load Factor

Occupant Load = 4600 GSF / 60 GSF = 76.6 = 77 occupants

or:

Occupant Load = 427.3 GSM / 5.574 GSM = 76.7 = 77 occupants

The expected number of 125 occupants falls within the maximum of 154 required by codes on the first floor. However, the 85 occupants on the second floor is above the 77 occupants allowed by the code Therefore, this building will not accommodate the desired occupant load. (*Note:* Strictly speaking, the building could not be used as intended by the owner. However, if a lower occupant load were acceptable on the second floor, then the building could house a Mercantile use.)

☐ CHAPTER 3: Construction Types and Building Sizes

PROBLEM 1

a. "A" designates a "protected" structure and "B" indicates an "unprotected" structure.

Explanation: Although it is not stated directly in the table, the "A" and "B" in this table indicate when further fire protection has been added to a structural system. This typically results in one additional hour of fire resistance rating of the structural components of the building. For example, you can see this by comparing Type IIIA to Type IIIB. (*Note:* Protected and unprotected do not have anything to do with whether the building has an automatic sprinkler system. See the discussion of protected and unprotected in Chapter 3 of the *Guidebook*.)

b. 1 hour.

> **Explanation:** Using *IBC* Table 601, find the column for Type V and the subcolumn for "A" (protected). When you cross-reference that to the row titled "Primary Structural frame," you will find that a 1-hour fire resistance rating is required for that building element.

c. 1 hour or the use of an automatic sprinkler system.

> **Explanation:** Using *IBC* Table 601, find the column for Type II and the subcolumn for "A" (protected). When you cross-reference that to the row titled, "Bearing walls, Interior," you will find that a 1-hour rating is required. However, if you refer to the note indicated at "A," you are told that an approved automatic sprinkler system can be substituted for the 1-hour fire resistance-rated construction.

d. Type 1, protected (A) or unprotected (B).

> **Explanation:** In *IBC* Table 601, "Floor construction and associated secondary members" is listed in the "Building Element" column. Compare the requirements for these elements for each of the construction types. Type I is the only construction type with a rating this high.

e. Interior nonbearing walls or partitions.

> **Explanation:** In *IBC* Table 601, locate "Nonbearing walls and partitions, Interior" under the "Building Elements" column. If you follow that row under all the construction types, you can see that no construction type requires a non(load)-bearing partition in the interior of a building to be rated. (*Note*: These partitions may be required to be rated for other reasons within the building codes, but not because of the construction type.)

PROBLEM 2

a. No, because this building type (R-1) cannot have more than 16,000 square feet (1486.4 sm) per floor under this type of construction; 17,500 square feet (1626 s m) exceeds the allowable amount.

> **Explanation:** Looking at the left side of *IBC* Table 503 under "Group," a hotel would fall under the Residential use group "R-1." (See Appendix A.1.) Under this category on the code table, a "Type IIIB" building cannot be more than 4 stories high with a maximum of 16,000 square feet (1486.4 sm) per floor. The number of stories in this existing building is allowable; the square footage is not. Although there are increases in area allowances in the codes if the building is sprinklered, this provision does not apply in this case.

b. No, because although the number of square feet is noted as "UL" (unlimited) for this use (R-3) and construction type, the code allows only three stories in this type of construction. (There are other factors to be considered as well.)

> **Explanation:** A townhouse or single-family home falls under the use group "R-3" on *IBC* Table 503. (See Appendix A.1.) When cross-referenced with construction "Type VB," R-3 requires the building to be no more than three stories. In this case, the townhouses that are planned to be four stories could not be built using Type VB construction. However, if you cross-reference this use with a more fire resistant construction type, you can see that the townhouses would be allowed to be constructed four stories high if at least Type III construction was used. (Type IV, Heavy Timber, would typically not be used in Residential occupancies.) Also notice that the townhouses that were planned to be three stories could be built using Type VB construction; however, they might be regulated by the *International Residential Code (IRC)* instead of the *IBC*. In all cases, the area is noted as unlimited for all construction types for R-3.

c. No, because the total square footage of the first floor of the existing building is more than what the code allows for this type of occupancy (F-2) in the existing construction type; 19,250 square feet (1788 sm) exceeds the maximum of 18,000 square feet (1672 sm) allowed by the code table.

> **Explanation:** If you calculate the number of square feet required for this factory using the occupant load formula, you will determine that your client's factory will require 10,000 square feet (929 sm):

$$\text{Occupant Load} = \text{Floor Area}/\text{Load Factor}$$

$$\text{Floor Area} = \text{Load Factor} \times \text{Occupant Load}$$

$$\text{Floor Area} = 100 \text{ GSF} \times 100 \text{ occupants} = 10,000 \text{ gross square feet}$$

or:

$$\text{Floor Area} = 9.29 \text{ GSM} \times 100 \text{ occupants} = 929 \text{ gross square meters}$$

Based on this alone, it looks like the space will work. However, in *IBC* Table 503, a low-hazard factory falls under "F-2." When you cross-reference with "Type IIIB," this category allows no more than three stories, with a maximum of 18,000 square feet (1672 sm) per story. The existing building has 19,250 gross square feet (1788 sm) on each floor, which is over the 18,000 square feet (1672 sm) allowed by the code. (*Note*: Increases in area allowed by the codes when an automatic sprinkler system is installed throughout the building may make this use possible.)

☐ CHAPTER 4: Means of Egress

PROBLEM 1

Most of these answers can be found in the various diagrams shown in Figures 4.5, 4.6, 4.7, and 4.8 of *The Codes Guidebook for Interiors*.

A. Riser height = 7 inches (178 mm) maximum (or 4–7 inches [100–178 mm])
B. Tread depth = 11 inches (279 mm) minimum
C. Nosing projection = $1\frac{1}{4}$ inches (38 mm) maximum
D. Stairway rise without landing = 12 feet (3658 mm) maximum
E. Height of handrail = 34–38 inches (864–965 mm)
F. Top handrail extension = 12 inches (305 mm) minimum
G. Bottom handrail extension = one tread depth. See the description of tread depth in answer B. (*Note*: Older editions of ADA and ICC A117.1 standards may require the extension to equal the depth of one tread plus 12 inches [305 mm].)
H. Diameter of Type I circular handrail = $1\frac{1}{4}$ to 2 inches (32–51 mm). This is the most common answer. There are two types of allowable handrail shapes: Type I and Type II. However, most handrails will typically be considered Type I. Although other shapes are allowed, the most common circular cross-section is required to meet this dimension.
I. Minimum headroom height = 80 inches (2032 mm)

PROBLEM 2

a. Basement = 2 exits
   First Floor = 4 exits
   Second Floor = 4 exits
   Third Floor = 4 exits
   Fourth Floor = 4 exits
   Fifth Floor = 3 exits
   Sixth Floor = 3 exits
   Seventh Floor = 3 exits
   Eighth Floor = 2 exits

Explanation: When determining the number of exits for an entire floor, remember that the quantity is also affected by the number of occupants on the floor(s) above. In this problem, the fourth floor had the highest occupant load (over 1000 = 4 exits). Since the number of exits cannot decrease as a person travels toward the exit discharge, there must be four exits on the third, second, and first floors as well (even though these floors by themselves do not need this many exits).

The fifth floor requires three exits (500 – 1000 = 3 exits). The sixth floor needs only two exits (1 – 500 = 2 exits). But since the seventh floor above requires three, the sixth floor requires three exits as well. The eighth floor is not affected by any other floor. The number of exits in the basement is not affected by the floors above, since it is below the main exit discharge at grade level. (Note, however, that when calculating the width of the exits, the occupant load of the basement may affect the exits on the first floor.)

b. 1. 250 feet (76,200 mm); using Table 1016.1.

Explanation: The restaurant on the first floor would be considered an Assembly (A-2) occupancy. (See Appendix A.1.) According to *IBC* Table 1016.1, in a sprinklered building, the maximum travel distance is 250 feet (76,200 mm).

2. 100 feet (30,480 mm); using Table 1021.1.

Explanation: Office spaces would be considered a Business (B) occupancy. Although Table 1016.1 allows a maximum of 300 feet (91,440 mm) as an allowable travel distance, *IBC* Table 1021.2(2) indicates that a first-story Business occupancy with a single exit is allowed a maximum of 75 feet (22,860 mm) with a minimum occupancy load of 49. In addition, you must refer to footnote "d," which states that if the building has an automatic sprinkler system, the maximum travel distance in a Group B occupancy is 100 feet (30,480 mm).

3. 250 feet (76,200 mm); using Table 1016.1.

Explanation: The wholesale retail shops would be considered a Mercantile (M) occupancy. For sprinklered buildings, *IBC* Table 1016.2 allows a maximum travel distance of 250 feet (76,200 mm).

4. 75 feet (22,860 mm); using Table 1021.2(2).

Explanation: The wholesale retail shops would be considered a Mercantile (M) occupancy. For a two-story building, *IBC* Table 1021.2(2) allows a maximum travel distance of 75 feet (22,860 mm) as long as the occupant load per floor is 29 or less.

5. 300 feet (91,440 mm); using Table 1016.1.

Explanation: The third through the seventh floors would be considered Business (B) occupancies. For sprinklered buildings, *IBC* Table 1016.2 allows a maximum travel distance of 300 feet (91,440 mm).

PROBLEM 3

a. 64 inches (1630 mm); 32 inches (815 mm).

Explanation: Even though the formula suggests that the total required width should be 26 inches (660 mm), and thus requires only $13\frac{1}{2}$ inches (343 mm) of width at each exit, the *IBC*, the NFPA codes, and accessibility regulations require all exit doors to provide at least a 32-inch (815-mm) clear opening. (This is typically accomplished with a door that is 36 inches [915 mm] wide.)

To determine the required exit width, you multiply the occupant load by the egress variable found on *LSC* Table 7.3.3.1. Since the telemarketing company is not a "Board and care," a "Health care," or "High hazard" occupancy, it would fall under the "All others" category. You can find the variable of 0.2 inches (5 mm) in the row noted as "All others" and in the columns "Level Components and Ramps."

Multiply this by the occupant load of 175, and you get 35 inches (875 mm). This is the total width required. Since two exits are required from the space, you divide the 35 inches (875 mm) of width between the two exit locations. This equals approximately 17.5 inches (437.5 mm) per exit door. However, the codes require a minimum of 32 inches (815 mm) for an exit in most occupancy classifications. (It is also the minimum required by the ADA and *ICC A117.1* standards.) In this case, a standard 36-inch (915-mm) door will provide a 32-inch (815-mm) clear opening in each location. (*Note:* Although the *IBC* provides different egress width factors for each type of use for a sprinklered and nonsprinklered space, the NFPA codes do not differentiate, except for Health care. In the NFPA code, the determining factors depend primarily on the use of the area, whether you are determining the width of a stairway or a level or ramp component).

b. 46 inches (1150 mm), because the calculated exit stair width is larger than the minimum exit stair width required by the codes.

Explanation: The exit stairs serve the entire floor, so to determine the calculated width, you must first determine the total occupant load for the floor. The occupant load for each space has been given on the plan in Figure 4.3:

$$36 + 50 + 175 + 45 = 306 \text{ total occupants}$$

Next, you need to look up the stair variable on *LSC* Table 7.3.3.1. Each of the spaces on this floor would be included in the "All others" category, so the variable of 0.3 inches (7.6 mm) for stairway width is used.

Multiply this variable by the total occupant load of 306 to get 91.8, or 92 inches (2325.6 mm). There are two stairways serving this floor, so this figure can be divided by two. The calculated minimum width for each stairway is 46 inches (1150 mm) wide. Although means of egress codes require a minimum stair width of 44 inches (1118 mm), the occupant load of this floor will require a larger width. In this case, the minimum requirement is determined by the calculated width, not the minimum width.

c. 44 inches (1118 mm), because even though the formula requires a corridor width of 30.5 inches (765 mm), the *IBC* and the NFPA codes require an exit access corridor to be a minimum of 44 inches (1118 mm).

Explanation: To determine the corridor width for the entire floor, you use the capacity factor variable for "Level Components and Ramps" of 0.2 inches (5 mm) (see Explanation to "a," above) and the total occupant load of 306 (see Explanation to "b," above). Multiply the total occupant load of 306 by the variable to get 61.2 inches (1530 mm). Since there are two stairways serving this floor, this number can be divided by two. So the calculated minimum width for the corridor is 30.6 inches (765 mm). However, from what you know about codes, you should recall that a 44-inch (1118-mm) minimum width is required for corridors. In this case, the minimum requirement will determine the required width, not the calculated width. (*Note:* Accessibility requirements would also require the corridors leading up to the exit stairs to be wider than 30.6 inches [765 mm] to allow the necessary clearance at the jamb side of the stairway doors. Wider turnaround areas may also be required.)

PROBLEM 4

Figure 4.4a is the same floor plan of the classroom/seminar room shown to scale at $\frac{1}{8}$"=1'-0". The various dimensions have been added to the plan for your use in calculating the aisle accessway widths.

a. 31 inches (787 mm); the minimum width of 12 inches (305 mm) for tables between 6 and 12 feet (1829 and 3658 mm) is added to the 19 inches (483 mm) required by codes for the chair.

Explanation: First, you must determine the length of Aisle Accessway A. (Remember that the length of the aisle accessway is measured to the middle of the last chair.) Using the $\frac{1}{8}$-inch scale, you can measure the length of the aisle accessway. It is approximately 8'-8" (2642 mm) long. At this length, according to the chart for an aisle accessway between the length of 6 and 12 feet (1829 and 3658 mm), the required minimum aisle width is 12 inches (305 mm). This is the distance between the chair back and the table edge. Because you were asked to give the minimum distance between the tables, this dimension is added to the 19-inch (483-mm) increment required in the codes to allow for the chair. (See Figure 5.2a.) Since 12 + 19 = 31 inches (305 mm + 483 mm = 788 mm), the total width required between the tables is 31 inches (788 mm).

b. 37 inches (940 mm); the calculated width of 18 inches (457 mm) is added to the 19 inches (483 mm) required by the codes for the chair.

Explanation: First, measure the length of the aisle accessway at Aisle Accessway B using your $\frac{1}{8}$-inch scale. (Remember, the length of the aisle accessway is measured to the middle of the last chair.) It is approximately 23'-" (7239 mm). Since the length of this row is between 12 and 30 feet (3658 and 9144 mm), the equation given in the chart for calculating the width of the aisle accessway must be used to determine the required aisle accessway width. In the equation, "*x*" is the length of the aisle accessway, which you have determined to be 23'-9" (7239 mm).

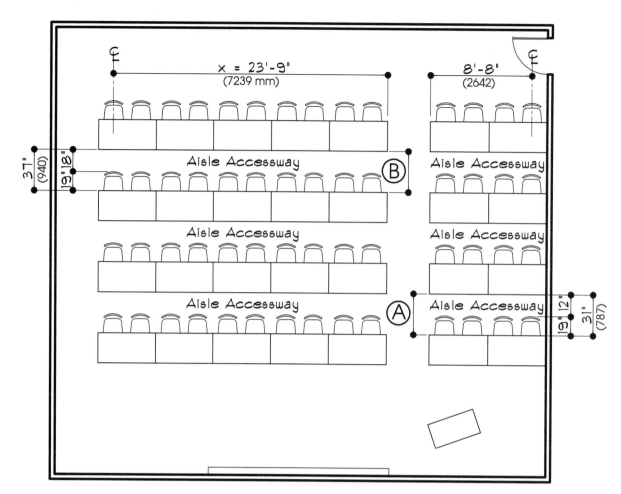

Figure 4.4a. Access Aisleway Widths: Training Room (Answer) (Scale: 1/8" = 1'-0").

$$12 \text{ inches} \times 0.5 \ (x - 12 \text{ feet})$$

$$12 \text{ inches} \times 0.5 \ (23'\text{-}9'' - 12 \text{ feet}) =$$

$$12 \text{ inches} \times 0.5 \ (11'\text{-}9'') =$$

$$12 \text{ inches} \times 0.5 \ (11.75 \text{ feet})$$

$$12 \text{ inches} \times 5.875 = 17.875 \text{ inches} = 18 \text{ inches} \ (454 \text{ mm})$$

You have been asked for the required minimum distance between the tables, so you must add this calculated width to the 19 inches (483 mm) required by the codes to allow for the chair. The minimum width required for this aisle accessway is 18 + 19 = 37 inches (940 mm). (*Note:* In the equation the 0.5 inches must be multiplied by the number of feet or a fraction thereof; 9 inches equals 0.75 feet [9 divided by 12].)

PROBLEM 5

Figure 4.5a is the same floor plan of the doctor's office shown to scale at ⅛' = 1'-0". The floor plan has been faded to the background so you can clearly see the answers. Each of the drawn lines has a different designation and is marked with the corresponding letter of the answer.

a. 34'-0" (10,363.2 mm), because the minimum required distance is half of the longest diagonal in the space.

Explanation: Using the half-diagonal rule, first you find the longest diagonal in the space using a straight line. This is shown by line A in the floor plan. If you use your ⅛-inch scale, the length of this line is 68'-0" (20,726.4 mm). Half of this line will give you the minimum distance required between the two exits. (*Note:* If the building had an automatic sprinkler system, the required separation distance might be reduced to one-third of the overall diagonal of the space.)

b. 67'-6" (20,574 mm) (This is accurate within 1 foot [305 mm].)

Explanation: Travel distance is defined as the maximum distance a person should have to travel from any position in a building or space to the nearest exit. To clearly show which travel distance is the longest, two have been measured on the floor plan in Figure 4.5a, each from the farthest corners from the exit. B1 starts in Exam 5 and B2 starts in Exam 2.

To measure the travel distance, start at the most remote point in the farthest corner of the room and draw straight lines along the centerline of the natural path of travel (i.e., centerline of the corridor). Take the most direct route to the exit, keeping at least 1 foot (305 mm) away from all walls and door jambs. Draw the lines to the centerline of each doorway, ending with the center of the exit door. After you draw all your lines, measure each straight line separately and put the dimensions directly on the floor plan. If you add up the dimensions for each line section, you get a travel distance for B1 of 68'-6" (20,574 mm) and B2 of 64'-0" (19,202.4 mm). Because B1 is the longest, it is the answer. (*Note:* All lines in this example are in 6-inch [150-mm] increments for ease of calculation.)

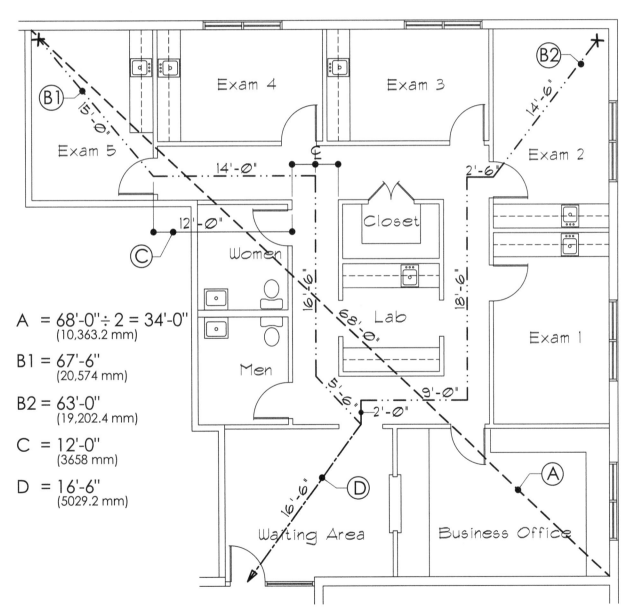

$$A = 68'-0'' \div 2 = 34'-0''$$
(10,363.2 mm)

$$B1 = 67'-6''$$
(20,574 mm)

$$B2 = 63'-0''$$
(19,202.4 mm)

$$C = 12'-0''$$
(3658 mm)

$$D = 16'-6''$$
(5029.2 mm)

Figure 4.5a. Travel Distance: Doctor's Office (Answer)
(Scale: 1/8" = 1'-0"; 1 Square Foot = 0.0929 Square Meter).

c. Yes; 12'-0" (3657.6 mm); Yes, because a dead-end corridor is typically allowed by the codes in a non-sprinklered building if it is less than 20 feet (6096 mm).

Explanation: A dead-end corridor is a corridor with only one direction of exit, which defines the corridor to Exam 5. To measure the dead-end corridor, start at the most remote point in the corridor, which in this case is at the door to Exam 5. Then follow the natural path of travel to where the corridor intersects the perpendicular corridor and where there are two directions to the exit. See the dimension line marked C on the floor plan. The distance is 12'-6" (3657.6 mm). (*Note:* The codes do not specify exactly how the travel distance is measured. Some AHJs may require the dead-end distance to extend to the centerline of the perpendicular corridor. In that case, the measured distance would be 14'-6" (4419.6 mm) but would still be within the allowable distance. In addition, if the building were sprinklered, a longer dead-end corridor length might be allowed.)

d. Yes; Waiting Area, 16'-6" (5029.2 mm).

Explanation: A common path of travel is defined as an exit access that is traveled before two separate options for exiting are available. It can also occur where two paths merge to become one, such as in the Waiting Area indicated by the letter D on the floor plan. It is where the two corridors merge on the way to the exit door. The length of the common path in the tenant space is within the allowable distance of 100' for an unsprinklered building as indicated in Table 1014.3.(See Figure A.8 in Appendix A)

CHAPTER 5: Fire and Smoke Resistant Assemblies

PROBLEM 1

Hourly Fire Resistance Rating of Wall Assemblies:

A. 0 hours (or no rating); using Table 508.4.

Explanation: This is an occupancy separation wall because it separates the Business (B) and Mercantile (M) occupancies. To determine the required rating, you must refer to *IBC* Table 508.4. Look under the "Occupancy" column to locate the row that includes "B" for Business. Then cross-reference this row with the column that includes "M" for Mercantile along the top of the table. The plan indicates that this building is nonsprinklered. So you will use the subcolumn indicating "NS" under the column containing "M." Where the row and the column meet, an "N" is shown. This means that no separation is required.

B. No rating; using Table 1018.1.

Explanation: Typically, fire resistance-rated walls are not required in small tenant spaces. However, to confirm this with the information in the code, refer to *IBC* Table 1018.1. The wall indicated on the plan is a corridor wall within the tenant space in a Business (B) use. Find "B" under the column for "Occupancy." You can see that the table only gives information for exit access corridors that serve an occupant load of more than 30. Because you are told that the occupant load is only 13, in this case the corridor walls would not be required to be rated.

C. 1-hour; using Table 1018.1.

Explanation: This is a corridor wall and is considered an exit access corridor. Refer to *IBC* Table 1018.1. Business (B) and Mercantile (M) occupancies are included in the same group under the "Occupancy" column. Because you can determine that the exit access corridor serves an occupant load of 91 (13 + 14 + 12 + 7 = 45) and you were told that the building is nonsprinklered, the corridor is required to have a fire resistance rating of 1 hour. (*Note:* If the building had been sprinklered, the exit access corridor would not have been required to be rated.)

D. 1-hour; using Table 1018.1.

Explanation: This is a corridor wall and is considered an exit access corridor. The same information as noted in item C preceding applies. (*Note:* Some jurisdictions may allow restroom walls to be nonrated.)

E. 2-hour; no code table.

Explanation: This wall is part of the fire barriers that enclose the elevator. An elevator wall is considered a type of shaft enclosure. From what you know about the codes, remember that the codes require elevator shafts to be rated 2 hours when they extend more than three floors. The portion of this enclosure that is part of the exit access corridor also must be rated 2 hours.

F. No rating; no code table.

Explanation: On the floor plan, you are told that the area of the storage room is 150 square feet (14 sm). However, when you refer to *IBC* Table 508.4, the column titled "Room or Area" has no listing for storage rooms or areas. (*Note:* In earlier editions of the *IBC*, this room would have been required to be rated 1 hour; however, that changed in the 2009 edition.)

G. 1-hour (or an automatic sprinkler system); using Table 508.4.

Explanation: Refer to *IBC* Table 508.4. In the column titled "Room or Area," you can find "Waste and linen collection rooms over 100 square feet." Since the area of this trash room is 120 square feet (11.1 sm), it is considered an incidental use. To determine the required rating, look at the column titled "Separation and/or Protection" to see that for this use, a 1-hour-rated wall is required. The table also tells you that an automatic extinguishing system within the room may be substituted for the rated walls.

H. 2-hour; no code table.

Explanation: This wall is part of the exit access corridor; however, it is also part of the exit stairway. Therefore, it is part of the fire barriers that enclose the exit stair. From what you know about the codes, remember that the codes require stairways to be rated 2 hours when they extend more than three floors. The portion of this enclosure that is part of the exit access corridor must also be rated 2 hours.

Hourly Fire Rating of Opening Protectives:

1. ⅓-hour (or 20-minute); using Table 716.5.

   Explanation: This door is located in the exit access corridor wall. You have already determined that the exit access corridor for this building requires a 1-hour rating. Now refer to *IBC* Table 716.5. Under the column for "Type of Assembly," find "Fire partitions, Corridor walls." Then, locate a 1-hour rating under the column "Required Wall Assembly Rating (hours)." Follow that over to the next column titled "Minimum Fire Door and Fire Shutter Assembly Rating (Hours)." You then find that a ⅓-hour rating is required. This is commonly referred to as a 20-minute door.

2. No rating; no code table.

   Explanation: Since the walls in the tenant space do not require a fire rating, neither do the doors located in these walls.

3. ⅓-hour (or 20-minute); using Table 715.4.

   Explanation: This door is located within the exit access corridor, which you have already determined to be rated 1 hour. The same information as noted in item 1 applies here. (*Note:* Some jurisdictions may allow restroom doors to be nonrated.)

4. 1½-hour; using Table 715.4.

   Explanation: This door is located in the stairway enclosure. You have already determined that the walls surrounding the stairway require a 2-hour rating. Now refer to *IBC* Table 716.5. Under the column titled "Type of Assembly," the first row is "Fire walls and fire barriers having a required fire-resistance rating greater than 1 hour." Find the 2-hour rating under "Required Assembly Rating (Hours)" and you can determine that a 1½-hour-rated door is required.

5. ⅓-hour (or 20-minute); using Table 715.4.

   Explanation: This door is located within the exit access corridor, which you have already determined to be rated 1 hour. The same information as noted in item 1 applies here. (*Note:* Some jurisdictions may allow restroom doors to be nonrated.)

6. 1½-hour; using Table 715.4.

   Explanation: This door is located in a shaft enclosure that is more than three stories. You have already determined that the walls surrounding this elevator require a 2-hour rating. The same information as noted in item 4 applies here.

7. ¾-hour; using Table 715.4.

   Explanation: Similar to item 3, this door is located in a wall that is an exit access corridor, which you have determined must be rated 1 hour. It is also part of the enclosure to an incidental use room, "Waste and linen collection rooms over 100 square feet." (For this example, we will assume that the option of providing an automatic extinguishing system is not being used.) Refer to *IBC* Table 716.5 to determine the rating of the door. Under "Type of Assembly," you find two options for interior walls rated 1 hour: "Fire barriers having a required fire-resistance rating of 1 hour" and "Fire partitions." From what you know about the codes, you recall that exit access corridor walls would be considered fire partitions; however, the walls enclosing the incidental use room would be considered fire barriers. Fire barriers have more stringent requirements than fire partitions. Because this wall does both, you must use the requirements for the fire barriers. The table lists two types of fire barriers. Because these walls do not enclose a shaft, stairway, ramp, or passageway, the "other fire barriers" is the correct type of fire barrier. You can then determine that a ¾-hour-rated door is required.

8. 1½-hour; using Table 716.5.

   Explanation: This plan indicates that this opening is within the actual refuse chute. This type of opening would be considered part of the shaft enclosure. Because we must assume that it extends through all the building floors, the shaft enclosure would require a rating of 2 hours, like the elevators and the stairway enclosures.

PROBLEM 2

a. 1-hour; No, an automatic sprinkler system is not required.

   Explanation: "Waste and linen collection rooms over 100 square feet" is a category shown toward the bottom of *IBC* Table 509. You were told that the area of the room is 250 square feet (23 sm), so these requirements would apply. This category requires a 1-hour fire rating. It does not require an automatic fire-extinguishing system if the fire resistance-rated partitions are provided. However, you could provide an automatic sprinkler system within the area instead of the rated partitions.

b. No.

   Explanation: Although storage rooms of more than 100 square feet were required to be rated in previous editions of the *IBC*, beginning in the 2009 *IBC*, they are no longer required to be separated, unless they become large enough to be considered a separate occupancy.

c. No, this is not allowed in I-2 occupancies.

   Explanation: A hospital is an I-2 occupancy classification according to the *IBC*. (See Figure A.1 in Appendix A.) The "Room or Area" designation for "Group I-2 waste and linen collection rooms" indicates that a 1-hour separation is required. It does not give you the option of an automatic sprinkler system instead of the rated partitions. (*Note:* This is because in most cases, hospitals are required to be sprinklered by the codes, so this would not provide any additional protection to this room.)

d. Yes; No

   Explanation: The science lab would fit under an Educational occupancy. (See Figure A.1 in Appendix A.) The room designation for "Laboratories and vocational shops, not classified as Group H, located in a

Group E or I-2 occupancy". This indicates that a 1-hour separation is required. It does give the option of using an automatic fire-extinguishing system instead of the rated partitions.

e. Laundry rooms and waste and collection rooms.

Explanation: In the table under "Room or Area," both room types must be more than 100 square feet before separation and/or protection is required by the *IBC*.

☐ CHAPTER 6: Fire Protection Systems

PROBLEM 1

Here we list 21 different automatic sprinkler "trade-offs" that affect interior spaces. Any of these is a possible answer. Many of these trade-offs were given in the "Common Sprinkler Trade-Offs" list in Figure 6.6 of the *Guidebook*. Others were mentioned within the text.

1. Lower fire ratings in walls and floor/ceiling assemblies

2. Longer travel distances

3. Larger areas of glazing

4. Reduced number of fire alarms

5. Lower finish class requirements

6. Lower furniture ratings

7. Eliminate firestops behind raised finishes

8. Additional foam plastic insulation or trim

9. Longer dead-end corridors

10. Open exit access stairways between two and three stories

11. Nonenclosed escalators

12. Omit or reduce rating of fire dampers

13. Reduce draftstops

14. Eliminate or reduce standpipes

15. Allow less fire resistant construction types

16. Reduce the number of fire extinguishers

17. Additional decorative trim

18. Less compartmentation in a high-rise building

19. Lower rating of opening protectives

20. Area of refuge may not be required at accessible elevators and exit stairways

21. Increase in allowable areas

PROBLEM 2

A. Upright

B. Recessed sidewall

C. Pendant

D. Recessed pendant

E. Concealed

F. Sidewall

☐ CHAPTER 7: Plumbing and Mechanical Requirements

PROBLEM 1

Most of these answers can be found in the various diagrams shown in Figures 7.2, 7.3, 7.5, 7.6, and 7.7 of the *Guidebook*. Other accessible toilet requirements are mentioned within the text. (*Note*: Although there may be some minor differences between the codes, the *ADA Standards*, and the *ICC A117.1* accessibility standard, you were asked to provide the most restrictive requirements based on the most current documents in each case.)

A. Depth of lavatory = 17–25 inches (430–635 mm)

B. Height of clear kneespace = 27 inches (685 mm) minimum

C. Height of clear toespace = 9 inches (230 mm) minimum

D. Height to top of lavatory = 34 inches (865 mm) maximum

E. Length of rear grab bar = 36 inches (915 mm) minimum

F. Distance from end of rear grab bar to centerline of toilet = 12 inches (305 mm) minimum

G. Height to grab bar = 33–36 inches (840–915 mm)

H. Height to top of toilet seat = 17–19 inches (430–485 mm)

I. Distance from centerline of toilet to side wall = 16–18 inches (405–455 mm)

J. Distance between centerline of toilet and centerline of lavatory = 30 inches (762 mm) minimum

K. Height to bottom of mirror = 40 inches (1015 mm) maximum (when above lavatory)

L. Distance from rear wall to side grab bar = 12 inches (305 mm) maximum

M. Length of side grab bar = 42 inches (1065 mm) minimum

N. Diameter of grab bar = 1¼ to 1½ inches (32–38 mm), or 1½ inch (38 mm) maximum

O. Height of vertical grab bar = 18 inches (455 mm) minimum

P. Distance from floor to bottom of vertical grab bar = 39–41 inches (990–1040 mm)

PROBLEM 2

a. 9 female, 9 male

Explanation: An elementary school is considered an Educational (E) occupancy in *IPC* Table 403.1. If you look for "Educational" under the column titled "Classification," there are no subclassifications. The ratio for water closets is "1 per 50."

As required by the *IPC*, you must first divide the total occupant load in half to determine how many fixtures are required for each sex. You are given the occupant load of 820. 820 divided by 2 =

410 for each sex. Then, take the 410 and divide it by the ratio of 50 to obtain 8.2 water closets. Note "a" at the bottom of the table indicates that you must round up for any fraction of a number of persons. Therefore, rounding up, this school requires 9 water closets for females and 9 water closets for males. (*Note*: If you had not first halved the total occupant load as the code now requires, you would have obtained a different result of 8 water closets for each sex.)

b. 12; the code requires 4 water closets for the visitors and 8 water closets for employees.

Explanation: A nursing home is listed in *IPC* Table 403.1 as an Institutional (I-2) occupancy. First, find "Institutional" under the column titled "Classification." Then locate "I-2" under the "Occupancy" column. Adjacent to I-2 you can see that there is a separate category for "Employees, other than residential care" and "Visitors, other than residential care" in the "Description" column.

First looking at the requirement for employees, you see that the water closet ratio is "1 per 25" occupants. You are given the total occupant load of 155, which the *IPC* requires to be divided in half before proceeding with the calculation. 155 divided by 2 = 77.5 occupants for each sex. Then, divide the 77.5 by the fixture ratio of 25 to obtain 3.1. Rounding up as required, there must be 4 female water closets and 4 male water closets for a total of 8 employee water closets. (*Note*: If you had not first halved the total occupant load as the code now requires, you would have obtained a different result. The total occupant load of 155 divided by 25 = 6.2. Rounding up, it would have resulted in a total of 7 water closets required for all employees. Also see Note "b," which states that employees must be provided with facilities separate from those for patients.)

Now, determine the requirements for visitors. The row in the table titled "Visitors, other than residential care" calls for 1 per 75 occupants. The total occupant load of 155 divided in half equals 77.5 divided by 75 = 1.03 for each sex. This number must also be rounded up. Thus, 4 water closets are required for all visitors. A total of 12 water closets (4 + 8) is required for employees and visitors.

c. 16 water closets (8 water closets for male and 8 water closets for female)

8 lavatories (4 lavatories for male and 4 lavatories for female)

2 drinking fountains

Explanation: Find "Assembly" under the "Classification" column in *IPC* Table 403.1. Nightclubs are listed as "A-2" in the "Occupancy" column. For Assembly occupancies, specific ratios are provided for water closets for each gender. (In this case, the ratio is equally distributed between genders, with 1 water closet required for every 40 occupants.) Per the *IPC*, the total occupant load of 600 should be divided in half, assuming there would be 300 males and 300 females. Then divide 300 by 40 to obtain 7.5. As instructed in Note "a" at the bottom of the table, you must round the number up to 8. So, 8 water closets must be provided for each gender.

For lavatories, the required ratio is 1 per 75: 600 divided by 75 = 8 total. (This would be distributed equally so that 4 lavatories would be for males and 4 lavatories for females.) For drinking fountains, the ratio is 1 per 500: 600 divided by 500 = 1.2. Since you need to round up, 2 drinking fountains must be provided. (To meet accessibility requirements, one should be mounted at standing height and one at wheelchair height. A "hi-lo" drinking fountain would also meet this requirement.)

d. None; no clothes washers are listed as being required in the table.

Explanation: A dormitory would be considered a Residential (R-2) occupancy. Find "Residential" and "R-2" under the "Classification" and "Occupancy" columns in *IPC* Table 403.1. Then find "Dormitories, fraternities, sororities, and boarding houses (not transient)" under the "Description" column. Under the column labeled "Other," only 1 service sink is required. An automatic clothes washer connection is not listed.

e. Three (3).

Explanation: An apartment building would be considered Residential (R-2). Find "Residential" and "R-2" in the "Classification" and "Occupancy" columns in *IPC* Table 403.1. For an "Apartment house," the requirements under "Other" indicate 1 automatic clothes washer connection per 20 dwelling units. So, 45 dwelling units divided by 20 = 2.25. Rounding up, 3 are required.

f. 1 water closet, 1 lavatory, 1 bathtub or shower, 1 kitchen sink, 1 automatic clothes washer connection.

Explanation: The requirements for a single-family dwelling are found in *IPC* Table 403.1 under Residential (R-3), "One- and two-family dwellings." Each required fixture is listed across the table in that row.

g. Females; females have a lower ratio and therefore require more water closets.

Explanation: An opera house would have an A-1 Assembly classification. The requirement for water closets for "Assembly" and "A-1" on *IPC* Table 403.1 is "1 per 125" for male and "1 per 65" for female; 65 will divide into the occupant load more often than the 125 for males, so the requirement for females is greater. (Sometimes these numbers can be amended by local laws. See the discussion of "potty parity" in Chapter 7 of the *Guidebook*.)

☐ CHAPTER 8: Electrical and Communication Requirements

PROBLEM 1

a. No.

Explanation: The *NEC* requires all outlets above the countertop in a dwelling unit kitchen, as well as other outlets that serve the countertop, to be GFCI-protected. Wall outlets at standard height are not included.

b. Yes.

Explanation: The *NEC* requires all wall outlets in commercial and institution kitchens to be GFCI-protected, not just those that serve the countertop.

c. Yes.

Explanation: The *NEC* requires that all outlets within 6 feet (1.8 m) of a sink be GFCI-protected. You were told that the coffee maker would be adjacent to the bar sink.

d. Yes.

Explanation: The *NEC* requires that all outlets in a sleeping room be AFCI-protected. This includes outlets for receptacles, light fixtures, and switches.

e. No.

Explanation: The *NEC* does not require any outlet that has GFCI protection (e.g., bathrooms, kitchens) to also have AFCI protection.

f. Yes.

Explanation: The *NEC* requires all outlets in public and employee restrooms to be GFCI-protected, not just the outlet near the lavatory.

PROBLEM 2

In each case, you would refer to the "Building Area Type" column on the left side of the *IECC* Table C405.5.2 to find the type that best fits the project and use the corresponding lighting power density value to complete the required calculations.

a. 49,800 watts per square foot (4626.42 watts per sm).

Explanation: Using the building area type "Motion Picture Theater," multiply the floor area of 41,500 square feet (3855.35 sm) by the LPD value of 1.2 W/ft².

b. Jewelry: 2.5 W/ft² (part of Retail Area 4)
   Clothing: 1.4 W/ft² (part of Retail Area 3)
   Sporting goods: 0.6 W/ft² (part of Retail Area 2)

   Explanation: Each of these categories is listed in a specific "Retail Area" in footnote "b." Once you know the retail area, refer to the sample calculation to find the corresponding wattage per square foot (sm) value.

c. Separate calculations must be made using the *IECC* table and footnote "b":
   1. **2,700 watts per square foot (250.83 watts per sm) for general lighting**
   2. **1,665 watts per square foot (154.68 watts per sm) for accent lighting at clothes and jewelry**

   Explanation: The women's clothing store would be considered "Retail" on the *IECC* table, which has an LPD value of 1.5 W/sf². Therefore, multiply the total floor area by 1.5 to obtain the wattage allowance for the general lighting. This building area type also refers you to footnote "b," which provides additional allowances for accent lighting. You determined in the previous question that clothing is part of "Retail Area 3" and jewelry is part of "Retail Area 4." These respective LPD values (see previous answer) are multiplied by the square footages (sm) provided for each area and are added together.

d. 3,100 watts per square foot (287.99 watts per sm).

   Explanation: Using the building area type "Office," multiply the floor area of 3,100 square feet (287.99 sm) by the LPD value of 1.0 W/ft². (The height of the ceiling is not part of the calculation.)

e. 107,050 watts per square foot (9,944.945 watts per sm); each use is considered a different building type, so they must be calculated separately using the appropriate LPD values and then added together.

   Explanation: Because there are two separate uses, each building area type is treated as a separate area. The building area type "Manufacturing Facility" with an LPD value of 1.2 W/ft² is used for the car manufacturing, and the building area type "Office" with an LPD value of 1.0 W/ft² is used for the corporate office. You multiply the floor area of 83,000 square feet (7710.7 sm) by the LPD value of 1.2 W/ft² and the floor area of 7,450 square feet (692.105 sm) by the LPD value of 1.0 W/ft²; then add the results.

☐ CHAPTER 9: Finish and Furniture Selection

PROBLEM 1

a. *Pill Test* (or *16 CFR 1630* or *DOC FF1–70* or *ASTM 2859*).

   Explanation: Any of these three answers would be correct. They are all the same test. (It is also known as the *Methenamine Pill Test*.) Federal law requires that all carpets sold in the United States pass this test. The *Flooring Radiant Panel Test would not* be the correct answer, because it is rarely required in a room or space that is not part of an exit or exit access.

b. *Room Corner Test* (or *NFPA 265* or *UL 1715*), because it is the standard test required by the codes for napped, tufted, or looped fabrics or carpets used on walls and ceilings.

c. *NFPA 701* (or *ASTM D6413*), because it is the standard test required by the codes for vertical treatments that hang straight, and this tapestry covers more than 10 percent of the wall area.

d. *NFPA 701* (or *ASTM D6413*), because it is the standard test required by the codes for vertical treatments that are folded or gathered.

e. *CAL 133* (or *ASTM E1537*), because it is the standard test required by the codes in public spaces with 10 or more seats when sprinklers are not present.

   Explanation: The *Life Safety Code* and *International Fire Code* require these tests in certain occupancies that are nonsprinklered. However, for both safety and liability reasons, you should always use the strictest finish and furniture requirements available, even if they are not currently required by a jurisdiction.

f. No test, because the "10 percent rule" typically allows small wall hangings to be nonrated.

   Explanation: If you wanted a rated wall hanging, it would have to pass *NFPA 701* (see answer to part "c" of this question).

g. There are two main choices; any two of the following combinations would be an appropriate answer.
   1. *Steiner Tunnel Test* (**or** *ASTM E84* **or** *UL 723* **or** *NFPA 255*)
   2. *Smolder Resistance Test* (**or** *NFPA 260* **or** *ASTM E1353* **or** *CAL 117*)

   Explanation: Other, more stringent tests are available that test the entire piece of furniture or furniture assembly (i.e., mock-up), but you were only asked for upholstery-related tests.

h. *Room Corner Test* (or *NFPA 265* or *UL 1715*), because it is the standard test required by the codes for napped, tufted, or looped fabrics or carpets used on walls and ceilings.

i. *16 CFR 1632* and *16 CFR 1633* (or *CAL 603*), because all mattresses sold in the United States are required by federal law to pass these two tests.

j. *ASTM E1590* (or *CAL 129*), because although all mattresses must pass government testing, additional tests are required by the codes in certain occupancies.

k. There are two possible answers:
   1. *Room Corner Test* (or NFPA 265 or UL 1715)
   2. *Steiner Tunnel Test* (or ASTM E84 or UL 723 or NFPA 255) in conjunction with the standard ASTM E2573, "Standard Practice for Specimen Preparation and Mounting of Site-Fabricated Stretch Systems."

PROBLEM 2

This hotel consists of a total of three different occupancy classifications: Residential (R), Business (B), and Assembly (A). Since this is an existing building, each will be classified as an existing occupancy. If you refer to the "Occupancy" column on the left side of *LSC* Table A.10.2.2, the hotel itself (i.e., room and suites) would be under "Hotels and Dormitories—Existing." The business offices on the floor plan would be listed under "Business and Ambulatory Health Care—Existing." The third occupancy is for the ballroom, which would be considered an Assembly occupancy. You were told in the floor plan that the occupancy load of the ballroom is 305, so it would be classified as "Assembly—Existing, >300 occupant load."

1. Main Lobby: Class A only and Class I or II.

   Explanation: Since the Main Lobby acts as an exit for all three occupancies, you need to look in the table under "Exits" for each occupancy and determine which has the strictest requirements. The "Assembly" occupancy is the strictest for the wall and ceiling finishes, with a Class A; therefore, it is the only one allowed. However, it does not require rated floor finishes. Only the "Hotels and Dormitories" occupancy requires rated floor finishes. Therefore, floor finishes can be either Class I or Class II.

2. Ballroom: Class A or B (no floor rating).

   Explanation: The ballroom is considered an Assembly occupancy. The ballroom is not an exit or an exit access; in the table under "Other Spaces" for "Assembly," therefore Class A or B is allowed. No floor rating is required. (The table shows "NA" for not applicable.)

3. Offices: Class A, B, or C (no floor rating).

   Explanation: In the table under "Other Spaces" for "Business and Ambulatory Health Care," Class A, B, or C is allowed. No floor rating is required.

4. Corridor: Class A or B and Class I or II.

   Explanation: Although it could be argued that this exit access corridor primarily serves the hotel rooms, any of the occupancies could use this corridor to exit. Therefore, you need to look in the table under "Exit Access Corridors" for all three occupancies and determine which has the strictest requirements. All three require Class A or B wall and ceiling finishes. Only the "Hotels and Dormitories" occupancy requires a rated floor finish of either Class I or II.

5. Single Room: Class A, B, or C (no floor rating).

   Explanation: In the table under "Other Spaces" for "Hotels and Dormitories," Class A, B, or C is allowed. No floor rating is required.

6. Suite: Class A, B, or C (no floor rating).

   Explanation: Similar to the Single Room, the Suite is found in the table under "Other Spaces" for "Hotels and Dormitories." Class A, B, or C is allowed, but no floor rating is required.

7. Vestibule: Class A only and Class I or II.

   Explanation: This is considered an exit or exit passageway. Like the corridor in item 4 of this question, any of the three occupancies could use this exit. Therefore, you need to look in the table under "Exits" for each occupancy and determine which has the strictest requirements. The "Assembly" occupancy allows only Class A wall and ceiling finishes. The "Hotels and Dormitories" occupancy requires Class I or II floor finishes.

8. Exit Stair: Class A or B and Class I or II.

   Explanation: This is also considered an exit; however, it is an exit for the floors above. You were told that all the other floors are strictly hotel rooms, so your answer is determined by the "Hotels and Dormitories" occupancy. For "Exits," the table requires Class A or B wall and ceiling finishes and Class I or II floor finishes.

PROBLEM 3

a. Class C; Yes.

   Explanation: Note 6 at the bottom of the table explains what is allowed when a building has an automatic sprinkler system. Basically, the code allows you to reduce the required finish class by one class rating. In Problem 1, you determined that the minimum wall finish required in the nonsprinklered Ballroom is a Class B. Therefore, with sprinklers, you can use a finish that is one class rating lower than shown in *LSC* Table A.10.2.2 and use a Class C.

b. Class A and Class I or II.

   Explanation: This is found in *LSC* Table A.10.2.2 under "Exits" in the occupancy category of "Hotels and Dormitories—New."

c. Class A or B.

   Explanation: A Gift Shop would be considered a Mercantile (M) occupancy. The answer is found in *LSC* Table A.10.2.2 under "Other Spaces" in the "Mercantile—New" occupancy.

d. Class B.

   Explanation: A hospital would be considered a Health Care occupancy in the NFPA codes. The answer is found in *LSC* Table A.10.2.2 under "Other Spaces" in the occupancy category of "Healthcare—Existing." It gives you a choice of Class A or Class B. Class B is the lowest rating.

e. Class I or II.

   Explanation: A juvenile detention facility would be considered a Detentional/Correctional occupancy in the NFPA codes. The answer is found in *LSC* Table A.10.2.2 under "Exits" in the occupancy category of "Detention and Correctional—Existing."

f. Class II.

   Explanation: Although you are typically allowed to use a lower rated finish when an automatic sprinkler system is used, as described in answer "a" to this question, sprinklers are mandatory in new "Detention and Correctional" occupancies, as noted in the "Occupancy" column of *LSC* Table A.10.2.2. The last sentence in Note 6 at the bottom of the table also tells you that the code portion allowing a lower finish to be used when the building is sprinklered does not apply to Detention and Correctional occupancies. So, Class II is the lowest level of floor finish allowed.

CHAPTER 10: Code Officials and the Code Process

There are no Study Problems for this chapter.

APPENDIX A

CODE TABLES

The code tables found in this appendix are also included in *Codes Guidebook for Interiors.* The corresponding figure number in the *Guidebook* is indicated under each table in this appendix.

Occupancy Classification	ICC *International Building Code*		NFPA *Life Safety Code and NFPA 5000*	
ASSEMBLY	A-1	Assembly, Theaters (Fixed Seats)	A	Assembly (variations noted by occupant load)
	A-2	Assembly, Food and/or Drink Consumption		
	A-3	Assembly, Worship, Recreation, Amusement		
	A-4	Assembly, Indoor Sporting Events		
	A-5	Assembly, Outdoor Activities		
BUSINESS	B	Business	B	Business
			AHC	Ambulatory Health Care
EDUCATIONAL	E	Educational (includes some day care)	E	Educational
FACTORY/INDUSTRIAL	F-1	Factory Industrial, Moderate Hazard	I	Industrial, General
	F-2	Factory Industrial, Low Hazard		Industrial, Special Purpose Industrial, High Hazard
HAZARDOUS	H-1	Hazardous, Detonation Hazard		(included in Group I)
	H-2	Hazardous, Deflagration Hazard or Accelerated Burning		
	H-3	Hazardous, Physical or Combustible Hazard		
	H-4	Hazardous, Health Hazard		
	H-5	Hazardous, Hazardous Production Materials (HPM)		
INSTITUTIONAL	I-1	Institutional, Custodial Care OL* >16	D-I	Detentional/Correctional (includes various subconditions I-V)
	I-2	Institutional, Medical Care	H	Health Care
	I-3	Institutional, Restrained (includes various subconditions I-5)	DC	Day Care
	I-4	Institutional, Day Care Facilities		
MERCANTILE	M	Mercantile	M-A	Mercantile, > 3 levels or > 30,000 SF (2800 SM)
			M-B	Mercantile, ≤ 3 stories or > 3000 SF (280 SM) and ≤ 30,000 SF (2800 SM)
			M-C	Mercantile, 1 story ≤ 3000 SF (280 SM)
RESIDENTIAL	R-1	Residential, Transient	R	Residential, Hotels and Dormitories
	R-2	Residential, Multi-Dwelling Unit		Residential, Apartment Buildings
	R-3	Residential, One and Two Dwelling Units		Residential, Lodging or Rooming Houses
				Residential, One- and Two-Family Dwellings
	R-4	Residential, Care and Assisted Living Facilities OL > 5 ≤16		Residential, Board and Care
STORAGE	S-1	Storage, Moderate Hazard	S	Storage
	S-2	Storage, Low Hazard		
UTILITY/ MISCELLANEOUS	U	Utility and Miscellaneous		Special Structures and High-Rise Buildings

Appendix A.1 Figure 2.2 Comparison of occupancy classifications. (This chart is a summary of information contained in the 2012 editions of the International Building Code®, the NFPA 5000®, and the Life Safety Code®. Neither the ICC nor the NFPA assumes responsibility for the accuracy or completeness of this chart.)

TABLE 1004.1.2
MAXIMUM FLOOR AREA ALLOWANCES PER OCCUPANT

FUNCTION OF SPACE	OCCUPANT LOAD FACTOR[a]
Accessory storage areas, mechanical equipment room	300 gross
Agricultural building	300 gross
Aircraft hangars	500 gross

Airport terminal
   Baggage claim
   Baggage handling
   Concourse
   Waiting areas
	
	20 gross
	300 gross
	100 gross
	15 gross

Assembly
   Gaming floors (keno, slots, etc.)
   Exhibit Gallery and Museum
	
	11 gross
	30 net

Assembly with fixed seats	See Section 1004.4

Assembly without fixed seats
   Concentrated (chairs only-not fixed)
   Standing space
   Unconcentrated (tables and chairs)
	
	7 net
	5 net
	15 net

Bowling centers, allow 5 persons for each lane including 15 feet of runway, and for additional areas	7 net
Business areas	100 gross
Courtrooms—other than fixed seating areas	40 net
Day care	35 net
Dormitories	50 gross

Educational
   Classroom area
   Shops and other vocational room areas
	
	20 net
	50 net

Exercise rooms	50 gross
Group H-5 Fabrication and manufacturing areas	200 gross
Industrial areas	100 gross

Institutional areas
   Inpatient treatment areas
   Outpatient areas
   Sleeping areas
	
	240 gross
	100 gross
	120 gross

Kitchens, commercial	200 gross

Library
   Reading rooms
   Stack area
	
	50 net
	100 gross

Locker rooms	50 gross
Mall buildings—covered and open	See Section 402.8.2

Mercantile
   Areas on other floors
   Basement and grade floor areas
   Storage, stock, shipping areas
	
	60 gross
	30 gross
	300 gross

Parking garages	200 gross
Residential	200 gross

Skating rinks, swimming pools
   Rink and pool
   Decks
	
	50 gross
	15 gross

Stages and platforms	15 net
Warehouses	500 gross

For SI: 1 square foot = 0.0929 m².

a. Floor area in square feet per occupant.

Appendix A.2 Figure 2.8 International Building Code (IBC) Table 1004.1.1, Maximum Floor Area Allowances per Occupant (2012 International Building Code, copyright 2012. Washington, DC: International Code Council. Reproduced with permission. All rights reserved. www.iccsafe.org).

BUILDING ELEMENT	TYPE I A	TYPE I B	TYPE II A[d]	TYPE II B	TYPE III A[d]	TYPE III B	TYPE IV HT	TYPE V A[d]	TYPE V B
Primary structural frame[g] (see Section 202)	3[a]	2[a]	1	0	1	0	HT	1	0

Bearing walls
  Exterior[f, g]
  Interior
	3
	3[a]
		2
		2[a]
			1
			1
				0
				0
					2
					1
						2
						0
							2
							1/HT
								1
								1
									0
									0

Nonbearing walls and partitions Exterior	See Table 602								
Nonbearing walls and partitions Interior[e]	0	0	0	0	0	0	See Section 602.4.6	0	0
Floor construction and associated secondary members (see Section 202)	2	2	1	0	1	0	HT	1	0
Roof construction and associated secondary members (see Section 202)	$1\frac{1}{2}$[b]	1[b,c]	1[b,c]	0[c]	1[b,c]	0	HT	1[b,c]	0

For SI: 1 foot = 304.8 mm.

a. Roof supports: Fire-resistance ratings of primary structural frame and bearing walls are permitted to be reduced by 1 hour where supporting a roof only.

b. Except in Group F-1, H, M and S-1 occupancies, fire protection of structural members shall not be required, including protection of roof framing and decking where every part of the roof construction is 20 feet or more above any floor immediately below. Fire-retardant-treated wood members shall be allowed to be used for such unprotected members.

c. In all occupancies, heavy timber shall be allowed where a 1-hour or less fire-resistance rating is required.

d. An approved automatic sprinkler system in accordance with Section 903.3.1.1 shall be allowed to be substituted for 1-hour fire-resistance-rated construction, provided such system is not otherwise required by other provisions of the code or used for an allowable area increase in accordance with Section 506.3 or an allowable height increase in accordance with Section 504.2. The 1-hour substitution for the fire resistance of exterior walls shall not be permitted.

e. Not less than the fire-resistance rating required by other sections of this code.

f. Not less than the fire-resistance rating based on fire separation distance (see Table 602).

g. Not less than the fire-resistance rating as referenced in Section 704.10

Appendix A.3 International Building Code Table 601, Fire-Resistance Rating Requirements for Building Elements (hours) (2012 International Building Code, copyright 2012. Washington, DC: International Code Council. Reproduced with permission. All rights reserved. www.iccsafe.org).

TABLE 503
ALLOWABLE BUILDING HEIGHTS AND AREAS[a, b]

Building height limitations shown in feet above grade plane. Story limitations shown as stories above grade plane.
Building area limitations shown in square feet, as determined by the definition of "Area, building," per story

GROUP		TYPE I A	TYPE I B	TYPE II A	TYPE II B	TYPE III A	TYPE III B	TYPE IV HT	TYPE V A	TYPE V B
HEIGHT (feet)		UL	160	65	55	65	55	65	50	40
		STORIES(S) / AREA (A)								
A-1	S	UL	5	3	2	3	2	3	2	1
	A	UL	UL	15,500	8,500	14,000	8,500	15,000	11,500	5,500
A-2	S	UL	11	3	2	3	2	3	2	1
	A	UL	UL	15,500	9,500	14,000	9,500	15,000	11,500	6,000
A-3	S	UL	11	3	2	3	2	3	2	1
	A	UL	UL	15,500	9,500	14,000	9,500	15,000	11,500	6,000
A-4	S	UL	11	3	2	3	2	3	2	1
	A	UL	UL	15,500	9,500	14,000	9,500	15,000	11,500	6,000
A-5	S	UL	UL	UL	UL	UL	UL	UL	UL	UL
	A	UL	UL	UL	UL	UL	UL	UL	UL	UL
B	S	UL	11	5	3	5	3	5	3	2
	A	UL	UL	37,500	23,000	28,500	19,000	36,000	18,000	9,000
E	S	UL	5	3	2	3	2	3	1	1
	A	UL	UL	26,500	14,500	23,500	14,500	25,500	18,500	9,500
F-1	S	UL	11	4	2	3	2	4	2	1
	A	UL	UL	25,000	15,500	19,000	12,000	33,500	14,000	8,500
F-2	S	UL	11	5	3	4	3	5	3	2
	A	UL	UL	37,500	23,000	28,500	18,000	50,500	21,000	13,000
H-1	S	1	1	1	1	1	1	1	1	NP
	A	21,000	16,500	11,000	7,000	9,500	7,000	10,500	7,500	NP
H-2	S	UL	3	2	1	2	1	2	1	1
	A	21,000	16,500	11,000	7,000	9,500	7,000	10,500	7,500	3,000
H-3	S	UL	6	4	2	4	2	4	2	1
	A	UL	60,000	26,500	14,000	17,500	13,000	25,500	10,000	5,000
H-4	S	UL	7	5	3	5	3	5	3	2
	A	UL	UL	37,500	17,500	28,500	17,500	36,000	18,000	6,500
H-5	S	4	4	3	3	3	3	3	3	2
	A	UL	UL	37,500	23,000	28,500	19,000	36,000	18,000	9,000
I-1	S	UL	9	4	3	4	3	4	3	2
	A	UL	55,000	19,000	10,000	16,500	10,000	18,000	10,500	4,500
I-2	S	UL	4	2	1	1	NP	1	1	NP
	A	UL	UL	15,000	11,000	12,000	NP	12,000	9,500	NP
I-3	S	UL	4	2	1	2	1	2	2	1
	A	UL	UL	15,000	10,000	10,500	7,500	12,000	7,500	5,000
I-4	S	UL	5	3	2	3	2	3	1	1
	A	UL	60,500	26,500	13,000	23,500	13,000	25,500	18,500	9,000
M	S	UL	11	4	2	4	2	4	3	1
	A	UL	UL	21,500	12,500	18,500	12,500	20,500	14,000	9,000
R-1	S	UL	11	4	4	4	4	4	3	2
	A	UL	UL	24,000	16,000	24,000	16,000	20,500	12,000	7,000
R-2	S	UL	11	4	4	4	4	4	3	2
	A	UL	UL	24,000	16,000	24,000	16,000	20,500	12,000	7,000
R-3	S	UL	11	4	4	4	4	4	3	3
	A	UL	UL	UL	UL	UL	UL	UL	UL	UL
R-4	S	UL	11	4	4	4	4	4	3	2
	A	UL	UL	24,000	16,000	24,000	16,000	20,500	12,000	7,000
S-1	S	UL	11	4	2	3	2	4	3	1
	A	UL	48,000	26,000	17,500	26,000	17,500	25,500	14,000	9,000
S-2	S	UL	11	5	3	4	3	5	4	2
	A	UL	79,000	39,000	26,000	39,000	26,000	38,500	21,000	13,500
U	S	UL	5	4	2	3	2	4	2	1
	A	UL	35,500	19,000	8,500	14,000	8,500	18,000	9,000	5,500

For SI: 1 foot = 304.8 mm, 1 square foot = 0.0929 m².

A = building area per story, S = stories above grade plane, UL = Unlimited, NP = Not permitted.

a. See the following sections for general exceptions to Table 503:

    1. Section 504.2, Allowable building height and story increase due to automatic sprinkler system installation.

    2. Section 506.2, Allowable building area increase due to street frontage.

    3. Section 506.3, Allowable building area increase due to automatic sprinkler system installation.

    4. Section 507, Unlimited area buildings.

b. See Chapter 4 for specific exceptions to the allowable height and areas in Chapter 5.

Appendix A.4. Figure 3.4 International Building Code (IBC) Table 503, Allowable Building Height and Areas (2012 International Building Code, copyright 2012. Washington, DC: International Code Council. Reproduced with permission. All rights reserved. www.iccsafe.org).

TABLE 1021.2(2)
STORIES WITH ONE EXIT OR ACCESS TO ONE EXIT FOR OTHER OCCUPANCIES

STORY	OCCUPANCY	MAXIMUM OCCUPANTS PER STORY	MAXIMUM EXIT ACCESS TRAVEL DISTANCE
First story or basement	A, B[b], E, F[b], M, U, S[b]	49 occupants	75 feet
	H-2, H-3	3 occupants	25 feet
	H-4, H-5, I, R-1, R-2[a,c], R-4	10 occupants	75 feet
	S	29 occupants	100 feet
Second story	B, F, M, S	29 occupants	75 feet
Third story and above	NP	NA	NA

For SI: 1 foot = 304.8 mm.

NP – Not Permitted

NA – Not Applicable

a. Buildings classified as Group R-2 equipped throughout with an *automatic sprinkler system* in accordance with Section 903.3.1.1 or 903.3.1.2 and provided with *emergency escape and rescue openings* in accordance with Section 1029.

b. Group B, F and S occupancies in buildings equipped throughout with an *automatic sprinkler system* in accordance with Section 903.3.1.1 shall have a maximum travel distance of 100 feet.

c. This table is used for R-2 occupancies consisting of *sleeping units*. For R-2 occupancies consisting of *dwelling units*, use Table 1021.2(1).

TABLE 1015.1
SPACES WITH ONE EXIT OR EXIT ACCESS DOORWAY

OCCUPANCY	MAXIMUM OCCUPANT LOAD
A, B, E, F, M, U	49
H-1, H-2, H-3	3
H-4, H-5, I-1, I-2, I-3, I-4, R	10
S	29

Appendix A.5 Figure 4.17 International Building Code Table 1015.1 Spaces with One Exit or Exit Access Doorway, Table 1021.2(1), Stories with One Exit or Access to One Exit for R-2 Occupancies, and Table 1021.2(2) Stories with One Exit or Access to One Exit for Other Occupancies, (2012 International Building Code, copyright 2012. Washington, DC: International Code Council. Reproduced with permission. All rights reserved. www.iccsafe.org).

TABLE 1016.2
EXIT ACCESS TRAVEL DISTANCE[a]

OCCUPANCY	WITHOUT SPRINKLER SYSTEM (feet)	WITH SPRINKLER SYSTEM (feet)
A, E, F-1, M, R, S-1	200	250[b]
I-1	Not Permitted	250[b]
B	200	300[c]
F-2, S-2, U	300	400[c]
H-1	Not Permitted	75[c]
H-2	Not Permitted	100[c]
H-3	Not Permitted	150[c]
H-4	Not Permitted	175[c]
H-5	Not Permitted	200[c]
I-2, I-3, I-4	Not Permitted	200[c]

For SI: 1 foot = 304.8 mm.

a. See the following sections for modifications to *exit access* travel distance requirements:

Section 402.8: For the distance limitation in *malls*.

Section 404.9: For the distance limitation through an *atrium* space.

Section 407.4: For the distance limitation in Group I-2.

Sections 408.6.1 and 408.8.1: For the distance limitations in Group I-3.

Section 411.4: For the distance limitation in special amusement buildings.

Section 1015.4: For the distance limitation in refrigeration machinery rooms.

Section 1015.5: For the distance limitation in refrigerated rooms and spaces.

Section 1021.2: For buildings with one *exit*.

Section 1028.7: For increased limitation in assembly seating.

Section 1028.7: For increased limitation for assembly open-air seating.

Section 3103.4: For temporary structures.

Section 3104.9: For pedestrian walkways.

b. Buildings equipped throughout with an *automatic sprinkler system* in accordance with Section 903.3.1.1 or 903.3.1.2. See Section 903 for occupancies where *automatic sprinkler systems* are permitted in accordance with Section 903.3.1.2.

c. Buildings equipped throughout with an *automatic sprinkler system* in accordance with Section 903.3.1.1.

Figure A.6 Figure 4.24 International Building Code Table 1016.1, Exit Access Travel Distance (2012 International Building Code, copyright 2012. Washington, DC: International Code Council. Reproduced with permission. All rights reserved. www.iccsafe.org).

Table 7.3.3.1 Capacity Factors

Area	Stairways (width/person) in.	Stairways (width/person) mm	Level Components and Ramps (width/person) in.	Level Components and Ramps (width/person) mm
Board and care	0.4	10	0.2	5
Health care, sprinklered	0.3	7.6	0.2	5
Health care, nonsprinklered	0.6	15	0.5	13
High hazard contents	0.7	18	0.4	10
All others	0.3	7.6	0.2	5

APPENDIX A.7 Figure 4.19 Life Safety Code Table 7.3.3.1, Capacity Factors (Reprinted with permission from NFPA 101®, Life Safety Code®, Copyright © 2011, National Fire Protection Association, Quincy, MA. This reprinted material is not the complete and official position of the NFPA on the referenced subject, which is represented only by the standard in its entirety.)

TABLE 508.4
REQUIRED SEPARATION OF OCCUPANCIES (HOURS)

OCCUPANCY	A, E		I-1ᵃ, I-3, I-4		I-2		Rᵃ		F-2, S-2ᵇ, U		B, F-1, M, S-1		H-1		H-2		H-3, H-4		H-5	
	S	NS	S	NS	S	NS	S	NS	S	NS	S	NS	S	NS	S	NS	S	NS	S	NS
A, E	N	N	1	2	2	NP	1	2	N	1	1	2	NP	NP	3	4	2	3	2	NP
I-1ᵃ, I-3, I-4	—	—	N	N	2	NP	1	NP	1	2	1	2	NP	NP	3	NP	2	NP	2	NP
I-2	—	—	—	—	N	N	2	NP	2	NP	2	NP	NP	NP	3	NP	2	NP	2	NP
Rᵃ	—	—	—	—	—	—	N	N	1ᶜ	2ᶜ	1	2	NP	NP	3	NP	2	NP	2	NP
F-2, S-2ᵇ, U	—	—	—	—	—	—	—	—	N	N	1	2	NP	NP	3	4	2	3	2	NP
B, F-1, M, S-1	—	—	—	—	—	—	—	—	—	—	N	N	NP	NP	2	3	1	2	1	NP
H-1	—	—	—	—	—	—	—	—	—	—	—	—	N	NP	NP	NP	NP	NP	NP	NP
H-2	—	—	—	—	—	—	—	—	—	—	—	—	—	—	N	NP	1	NP	1	NP
H-3, H-4	—	—	—	—	—	—	—	—	—	—	—	—	—	—	—	—	1ᵈ	NP	1	NP
H-5	—	—	—	—	—	—	—	—	—	—	—	—	—	—	—	—	—	—	N	NP

S = Buildings equipped throughout with an automatic sprinkler system installed in accordance with Section 903.3.1.1.

NS = Buildings not equipped throughout with an automatic sprinkler system installed in accordance with Section 903.3.1.1.

N = No separation requirement.

NP = Not permitted.

a See Section 420.

b. The required separation from areas used only for private or pleasure vehicles shall be reduced by 1 hour but to not less than 1 hour.

c. See Section 406.3.4.

d. Separation is not required between occupancies of the same classification.

Figure A.8 Figure 5.6 International Building Code Table 508.4, Required Separation of Occupancies (Hours) (2012 International Building Code, copyright 2012. Washington, DC: International Code Council. Reproduced with permission. All rights reserved. www.iccsafe.org).

TABLE 509
INCIDENTAL USES

ROOM OR AREA	SEPARATION AND/OR PROTECTION
Furnace room where any piece of equipment is over 400,000 Btu per hour input	1 hour or provide automatic sprinkler system
Rooms with boilers where the largest piece of equipment is over 15 psi and 10 horsepower	1 hour or provide automatic sprinkler system
Refrigerant machinery room	1 hour or provide automatic sprinkler system
Hydrogen cutoff rooms, not classified as Group H	1 hour in Group B, F, M, S and U occupancies; 2 hours in Group A, E, I and R occupancies.
Incinerator rooms	2 hours and provide automatic sprinkler system
Paint shops, not classified as Group H, located in occupancies other than Group F	2 hours; or 1 hour and provide automatic sprinkler system
Laboratories and vocational shops, not classified as Group H, located in a Group E or I-2 occupancy	1 hour or provide automatic sprinkler system
Laundry rooms over 100 square feet	1 hour or provide automatic sprinkler system
Group I-3 cells equipped with padded surfaces	1 hour
Waste and linen collection rooms located in either Group I-2 occupancies or ambulatory care facilities	1 hour
Waste and linen collection rooms over 100 square feet	1 hour or provide automatic sprinkler system
Stationary storage battery systems having a liquid electrolyte capacity of more than 50 gallons for flooded lead-acid, nickel cadmium or VRLA, or more than 1,000 pounds for lithium-ion and lithium metal polymer used for facility standby power, emergency power or uninterruptable power supplies	1 hour in Group B, F, M, S and U occupancies; 2 hours in Group A, E, I and R occupancies.

For SI: 1 square foot = 0.0929 m², 1 pound per square inch (psi) = 6.9 kPa, 1 British thermal unit (Btu) per hour = 0.293 watts, 1 horsepower = 746 watts, 1 gallon = 3.785 L.

APPENDIX A.9 Figure 5.8 International Building Code Table 509, Incidental Uses (2012 International Building Code, copyright 2012. Washington, DC: International Code Council. Reproduced with permission. All rights reserved. www.iccsafe.org).

TABLE 1018.1
CORRIDOR FIRE-RESISTANCE RATING

		REQUIRED FIRE-RESISTANCE RATING (hours)	
OCCUPANCY	OCCUPANT LOAD SERVED BY CORRIDOR	Without sprinkler system	With sprinkler system[c]
H-1, H-2, H-3	All	Not Permitted	1
H-4, H-5	Greater than 30	Not Permitted	1
A, B, E, F, M, S, U	Greater than 30	1	0
R	Greater than 10	Not Permitted	0.5
I-2[a], I-4	All	Not Permitted	0
I-1, I-3	All	Not Permitted	1[b]

a. For requirements for occupancies in Group I-2, see Sections 407.2 and 407.3.

b. For a reduction in the *fire-resistance rating* for occupancies in Group I-3, see Section 408.8.

c. Buildings equipped throughout with an *automatic sprinkler system* in accordance with Section 903.3.1.1 or 903.3.1.2 where allowed.

APPENDIX A.10 Figure 5.11 International Building Code Table 1018.1, Corridor Fire-Resistance Rating (2012 International Building Code, copyright 2012. Washington, DC: International Code Council. Reproduced with permission. All rights reserved. www.iccsafe.org).

TABLE 716.5
OPENING FIRE PROTECTION ASSEMBLIES, RATINGS AND MARKINGS

TYPE OF ASSEMBLY	REQUIRED WALL ASSEMBLY RATING (hours)	MINIMUM FIRE DOOR AND FIRE SHUTTER ASSEMBLY RATING (hours)	DOOR VISION PANEL SIZE	FIRE RATED GLAZING MARKING DOOR VISION PANEL[e]	MINIMUM SIDELIGHT/ TRANSOM ASSEMBLY RATING (hours)		FIRE-RATED GLAZING MARKING SIDELITE/TRANSOM PANEL	
					Fire protection	Fire resistance	Fire protection	Fire resistance
Fire walls and fire barriers having a required fire-resistance rating greater than 1 hour	4	3	Not Permitted	Not Permitted	Not Permitted	4	Not Permitted	W-240
	3	3[a]	Not Permitted	Not Permitted	Not Permitted	3	Not Permitted	W-180
	2	$1^1/_2$	100 sq. in.[c]	≤100 sq.in. = D-H-90 >100 sq.in.= D-H-W-90	Not Permitted	2	Not Permitted	W-120
	$1^1/_2$	$1^1/_2$	100 sq. in.[c]	≤100 sq.in. = D-H-90 >100 sq.in.= D-H-W-90	Not Permitted	$1^1/_2$	Not Permitted	W-90
Shaft, exit enclosures and exit passageway walls	2	$1^1/_2$	100 sq. in.[c, d]	≤100 sq.in. = D-H-90 > 100 sq.in.= D-H-T-or D-H-T-W-90	Not Permitted	2	Not Permitted	W-120
Fire barriers having a required fire-resistance rating of 1 hour: Enclosures for shafts, exit access stairways, exit access ramps, interior exit stairways, interior exit ramps and exit passageway walls	1	1	100 sq. in.[c, d]	≤100 sq.in. = D-H-60 >100 sq.in.= D-H-T-60 or D-H-T-W-60	Not Permitted	1	Not Permitted	W-60
				Fire protection				
Other fire barriers	1	$^3/_4$	Maximum size tested	D-H-NT-45	$^3/_4$		D-H-NT-45	
Fire partitions: Corridor walls	1	$^1/_3$[b]	Maximum size tested	D-20	$^3/_4$[b]		D-H-OH-45	
	0.5	$^1/_3$[b]	Maximum size tested	D-20	$^1/_3$		D-H-OH-20	
Other fire partitions	1	$^3/_4$	Maximum size tested	D-H-45	$^3/_4$		D-H-45	
	0.5	$^1/_3$	Maximum size tested	D-H-20	$^1/_3$		D-H-20	
Exterior walls	3	$1^1/_2$	100 sq. in.[c]	≤100 sq.in. = D-H-90 >100 sq.in = D-H-W-90	Not Permitted	3	Not Permitted	W-180
	2	$1^1/_2$	100 sq. in.[c]	≤100 sq.in. = D-H-90 >100 sq.in.= D-H-W-90	Not Permitted	2	Not Permitted	W-120
				Fire Protection				
	1	$^3/_4$	Maximum size tested	D-H-45	$^3/_4$		D-H-45	
Smoke barriers				**Fire protection**				
	1	$^1/_3$[b]	Maximum size tested	D-20	$^3/_4$		D-H-OH-45	

For SI: 1 square inch = 645.2 mm.

a. Two doors, each with a fire protection rating of $1^1/_2$ hours, installed on opposite sides of the same opening in a fire wall, shall be deemed equivalent in fire protection rating to one 3-hour fire door.

b. For testing requirements, see Section 716.5.3.

c. Fire-resistance-rated glazing tested to ASTM E 119 in accordance with Section 716.2 shall be permitted, in the maximum size tested.

d. Except where the building is equipped throughout with an automatic sprinkler and the fire-rated glazing meets the criteria established in Section 716.5.5.

e. Under the column heading "Fire-rated glazing marking door vision panel," W refers to the fire-resistance rating of the glazing, not the frame.

APPENDIX A.11 Figure 5.12 International Building Code Table 716.5, (2012 International Building Code, copyright 2012. Washington, DC: International Code Council. Reproduced with permission. All rights reserved. www.iccsafe.org).

TABLE 716.3
MARKING FIRE-RATED GLAZING ASSEMBLIES

FIRE TEST STANDARD	MARKING	DEFINITION OF MARKING
ASTM E 119 or UL 263	W	Meets wall assembly criteria.
NFPA 257 or UL 9	OH	Meets fire window assembly criteria including the hose stream test.
NFPA 252 or UL 10B or UL 10C	D	Meets fire door assembly criteria.
	H	Meets fire door assembly "Hose Stream" test.
	T	Meets 450°F temperature rise criteria for 30 minutes
	XXX	The time in minutes of the fire resistance or fire protection rating of the glazing assembly

For SI: °C = [(°F) - 32]/1.8.

APPENDIX A.11 (*Continued*)

TABLE 717.3.2.1
FIRE DAMPER RATING

TYPE OF PENETRATION	MINIMUM DAMPER RATING (hours)
Less than 3-hour fire-resistance-rated assemblies	1.5
3-hour or greater fire-resistance-rated assemblies	3

Figure A.12 Figure 5.16 International Building Code Table 717.3.2.1, Fire Damper Rating (2012 International Building Code, copyright 2012. Washington, DC: International Code Council. Reproduced with permission. All rights reserved. www.iccsafe.org).

NO.	CLASSIFICATION	OCCUPANCY	DESCRIPTION	WATER CLOSETS (URINALS SEE SECTION 419.2)		LAVATORIES		BATHTUBS/ SHOWERS	DRINKING FOUNTAINᵉ·ᶠ (SEE SECTION 410.1)	OTHER
				MALE	FEMALE	MALE	FEMALE			
1	Assembly	A-1ᵈ	Theaters and other buildings for the performing arts and motion pictures	1 per 125	1 per 65	1 per 200		—	1 per 500	1 service sink
		A-2ᵈ	Nightclubs, bars, taverns, dance halls and buildings for similar purposes	1 per 40	1 per 40	1 per 75		—	1 per 500	1 service sink
			Restaurants, banquet halls and food courts	1 per 75	1 per 75	1 per 200		—	1 per 500	1 service sink
		A-3ᵈ	Auditoriums without permanent seating, art galleries, exhibition halls, museums, lecture halls, libraries, arcades and gymnasiums	1 per 125	1 per 65	1 per 200		—	1 per 500	1 service sink
			Passenger terminals and transportation facilities	1 per 500	1 per 500	1 per 750		—	1 per 1,000	1 service sink
			Places of worship and other religious services.	1 per 150	1 per 75	1 per 200		—	1 per 1,000	1 service sink
1	Assembly	A-4	Coliseums, arenas, skating rinks, pools and tennis courts for indoor sporting events and activities	1 per 75 for the first 1,500 and 1 per 120 for the remainder exceeding 1,500	1 per 40 for the first 1,520 and 1 per 60 for the remainder exceeding 1,520	1 per 200	1 per 150	—	1 per 1,000	1 service sink
		A-5	Stadiums, amusement parks, bleachers and grandstands for outdoor sporting events and activities	1 per 75 for the first 1,500 and 1 per 120 for the remainder exceeding 1,500	1 per 40 for the first 1,520 and 1 per 60 for the remainder exceeding 1,520	1 per 200	1 per 150	—	1 per 1,000	1 service sink
2	Business	B	Buildings for the transaction of business, professional services, other services involving merchandise, office buildings, banks, light industrial and similar uses	1 per 25 for the first 50 and 1 per 50 for the remainder exceeding 50		1 per 40 for the first 80 and 1 per 80 for the remainder exceeding 80		—	1 per 100	1 service sinkᵍ
3	Educational	E	Educational facilities	1 per 50		1 per 50		—	1 per 100	1 service sink
4	Factory and industrial	F-1 and F-2	Structures in which occupants are engaged in work fabricating, assembly or processing of products or materials	1 per 100		1 per 100		(see Section 411)	1 per 400	1 service sink
		I-1	Residential care	1 per 10		1 per 10		1 per 8	1 per 100	1 service sink
			Hospitals, ambulatory nursing home care recipient	1 per roomᶜ		1 per roomᶜ		1 per 15	1 per 100	1 service sink per floor

APPENDIX A.13 Figure 7.1 International Plumbing Code® (IPC®) Table 403.1, Minimum Number of Required Plumbing Fixtures (2012 International Plumbing Code, copyright 2012. Washington, DC: International Code Council. Reproduced with permission. All rights reserved. www.iccsafe.org).

NO.	CLASSIFICATION	OCCUPANCY	DESCRIPTION	WATER CLOSETS (URINALS SEE SECTION 419.2)		LAVATORIES		BATHTUBS/ SHOWERS	DRINKING FOUNTAIN[e,f] (SEE SECTION 410.1)	OTHER
				MALE	FEMALE	MALE	FEMALE			
5	Institutional	I-2	Employees, other than residential care[b]	1 per 25		1 per 35		—	1 per 100	—
			Visitors, other than residential care	1 per 75		1 per 100		—	1 per 500	—
		I-3	Prisons[b]	1 per cell		1 per cell		1 per 15	1 per 100	1 service sink
			Reformitories, detention centers, and correctional centers[b]	1 per 15		1 per 15		1 per 15	1 per 100	1 service sink
			Employees[b]	1 per 25		1 per 35		—	1 per 100	—
		I-4	Adult day care and child day care	1 per 15		1 per 15		1	1 per 100	1 service sink
6	Mercantile	M	Retail stores, service stations, shops, salesrooms, markets and shopping centers	1 per 500		1 per 750		—	1 per 1,000	1 service sink[g]
7	Residential	R-1	Hotels, motels, boarding houses (transient)	1 per sleeping unit		1 per sleeping unit		1 per sleeping unit	—	1 service sink
		R-2	Dormitories, fraternities, sororities and boarding houses (not transient)	1 per 10		1 per 10		1 per 8	1 per 100	1 service sink
		R-2	Apartment house	1 per dwelling unit		1 per dwelling unit		1 per dwelling unit	—	1 kitchen sink per dwelling unit; 1 automatic clothes washer connection per 20 dwelling units
		R-3	Congregate living facilities with 16 or fewer persons	1 per 10		1 per 10		1 per 8	1 per 100	1 service sink
		R-3	One- and two-family dwellings	1 per dwelling unit		1 per dwelling unit		1 per dwelling unit	—	1 kitchen sink per dwelling unit; 1 automatic clothes washer connection per dwelling unit
		R-4	Congregate living facilities with 16 or fewer persons	1 per 10		1 per 10		1 per 8	1 per 100	1 service sink
8	Storage	S-1 S-2	Structures for the storage of goods, warehouses, storehouse and freight depots. Low and Moderate Hazard.	1 per 100		1 per 100		See Section411	1 per 1,000	1 service sink

a. The fixtures shown are based on one fixture being the minimum required for the number of persons indicated or any fraction of the number of persons indicated. The number of occupants shall be determined by the *International Building Code*.

b. Toilet facilities for employees shall be separate from facilities for inmates or care recipients.

c. A single-occupant toilet room with one water closet and one lavatory serving not more than two adjacent patient sleeping units shall be permitted where such room is provided with direct access from each patient sleeping unit and with provisions for privacy.

d. The occupant load for seasonal outdoor seating and entertainment areas shall be included when determining the minimum number of facilities required.

e. The minimum number of required drinking fountains shall comply with Table 403.1 and Chapter 11 of the *International Building Code*.

f. Drinking fountains are not required for an occupant load of 15 or fewer.

g. For business and mercantile occupancies with an occupant load of 15 or fewer, service sinks shall not be required.

APPENDIX A.13 (*Continued*)

TABLE 505.5.2
INTERIOR LIGHTING POWER ALLOWANCES

Building Area Type[a]	LIGHTING POWER DENSITY (W/ft²)
Automotive Facility	0.9
Convention Center	1.2
Court House	1.2
Dining: Bar Lounge/Leisure	1.3
Dining: Cafeteria/Fast Food	1.4
Dining: Family	1.6
Dormitory	1.0
Exercise Center	1.0
Gymnasium	1.1
Healthcare—clinic	1.0
Hospital	1.2
Hotel	1.0
Library	1.3
Manufacturing Facility	1.3
Motel	1.0
Motion Picture Theater	1.2
Multifamily	0.7
Museum	1.1
Office	1.0
Parking Garage	0.3
Penitentiary	1.0
Performing Arts Theater	1.6
Police/Fire Station	1.0
Post Office	1.1
Religious Building	1.3
Retail[b]	1.5
School/University	1.2
Sports Arena	1.1
Town Hall	1.1
Transportation	1.0
Warehouse	0.8
Workshop	1.4

For SI: 1 foot = 304.8 mm, 1 watt per square foot = W/0.0929 m².

a. In cases where both a general building area type and a more specific building area type are listed, the more specific building area type shall apply.

b. Where lighting equipment is specified to be installed to highlight specific merchandise in addition to lighting equipment specified for general lighting and is switched or dimmed on circuits different from the circuits for general lighting, the smaller of the actual wattage of the lighting equipment installed specifically for merchandise, or additional lighting power as determined below shall be added to the interior lighting power determined in accordance with this line item.

Calculate the additional lighting power as follows:

Additional Interior Lighting Power Allowance = 1000 watts + (Retail Area 1 × 0.6 W/ft²) + (Retail Area 2 × 0.6W/ft²) + (Retail Area 3 × 1.4 W/ft²) + (Retail Area 4 × 2.5 W/ft²).

where:

Retail Area 1 = The floor area for all products not listed in Retail Area 2, 3 or 4.

Retail Area 2 = The floor area used for the sale of vehicles, sporting goods and small electronics.

Retail Area 3 = The floor area used for the sale of furniture, clothing, cosmetics and artwork.

Retail Area 4 = The floor area used for the sale of jewelry, crystal and china.

Exception: Other merchandise categories are permitted to be included in Retail Areas 2 through 4 above, provided that justification documenting the need for additional lighting power based on visual inspection, contrast, or other critical display is *approved* by the authority having jurisdiction.

Appendix A.14 Figure 8.7 International Energy Conservation Code® Table 505.5.2, Interior Lighting Power Allowances (2012 International Energy Conservation Code, copyright 2012. Washington, DC: International Code Council. Reproduced with permission. Reproduced with permission. All rights reserved. www.iccsafe.org).

Table A.10.2.2 Interior Finish Classification Limitations

Occupancy	Exits	Exit Access Corridors	Other Spaces
Assembly — New			
>300 occupant load	A	A or B	A or B
	I or II	I or II	NA
≤300 occupant load	A	A or B	A, B, or C
	I or II	I or II	NA
Assembly — Existing			
>300 occupant load	A	A or B	A or B
≤300 occupant load	A	A or B	A, B, or C
Educational — New	A	A or B	A or B; C on low partitions[†]
	I or II	I or II	NA
Educational — Existing	A	A or B	A, B, or C
Day-Care Centers — New	A	A	A or B
	I or II	I or II	NA
Day-Care Centers — Existing	A or B	A or B	A or B
Day-Care Homes — New	A or B	A or B	A, B, or C
	I or II		NA
Day-Care Homes — Existing	A or B	A, B, or C	A, B, or C
Health Care — New	A	A	A
	NA	B on lower portion of corridor wall[†]	B in small individual rooms[†]
	I or II	I or II	NA
Health Care — Existing	A or B	A or B	A or B
Detention and Correctional — New	A or B	A or B	A, B, or C
(sprinklers mandatory)	I or II	I or II	NA
Detention and Correctional — Existing	A or B	A or B	A, B, or C
	I or II	I or II	NA
One- and Two-Family Dwellings and Lodging or Rooming Houses	A, B, or C	A, B, or C	A, B, or C
Hotels and Dormitories — New	A	A or B	A, B, or C
	I or II	I or II	NA
Hotels and Dormitories — Existing	A or B	A or B	A, B, or C
	I or II[†]	I or II[†]	NA
Apartment Buildings — New	A	A or B	A, B, or C
	I or II	I or II	NA
Apartment Buildings — Existing	A or B	A or B	A, B, or C
	I or II[†]	I or II[†]	NA
Residential Board and Care — *(See Chapters 32 and 33.)*			
Mercantile — New	A or B	A or B	A or B
	I or II		NA
Mercantile — Existing			
Class A or Class B stores	A or B	A or B	Ceilings — A or B; walls — A, B, or C
Class C stores	A, B, or C	A, B, or C	A, B, or C
Business and Ambulatory Health Care — New	A or B	A or B	A, B, or C
	I or II		NA
Business and Ambulatory Health Care — Existing	A or B	A or B	A, B, or C
Industrial	A or B	A, B, or C	A, B, or C
	I or II	I or II	NA
Storage	A or B	A, B, or C	A, B, or C
	I or II		NA

NA: Not applicable.

Notes:

(1) Class A interior wall and ceiling finish — flame spread index, 0–25 (new applications); smoke developed index, 0–450.

(2) Class B interior wall and ceiling finish — flame spread index, 26–75 (new applications); smoke developed index, 0–450.

(3) Class C interior wall and ceiling finish — flame spread index, 76–200 (new applications); smoke developed index, 0–450.

(4) Class I interior floor finish — critical radiant flux, not less than 0.45 W/cm².

(5) Class II interior floor finish — critical radiant flux, not more than 0.22 W/cm², but less than 0.45 W/cm².

(6) Automatic sprinklers — where a complete standard system of automatic sprinklers is installed, interior wall and ceiling finish with a flame spread rating not exceeding Class C is permitted to be used in any location where Class B is required, and Class B interior wall and ceiling finish is permitted to be used in any location where Class A is required; similarly, Class II interior floor finish is permitted to be used in any location where Class I is required, and no interior floor finish classification is required where Class II is required. These provisions do not apply to new detention and correctional occupancies.

(7) Exposed portions of structural members complying with the requirements for heavy timber construction are permitted.

[†]See corresponding chapters for details.

Appendix A.15 Figure 9.13 Life Safety Code Table A.10.2.2, Interior Finish Classification Limitations (Reprinted with permission from NFPA 101®, Life Safety Code®, Copyright © 2012, National Fire Protection Association, Quincy, MA. This reprinted material is not the complete and official position of the NFPA on the referenced subject, which is represented only by the standard in its entirety.)

APPENDIX B

FULL-SIZE CHECKLISTS

Each chapter (except Chapter 3) in *Codes Guidebook for Interiors* has a codes checklist. These same checklists have been reprinted in this appendix. The full-size format will make them easier to use. You may copy them, revise them, and use them for your various design projects.

For an explanation of how to use the checklists, refer to the *Guidebook.* They can be found at the end of each chapter in the *Guidebook.*

Interior Codes and Standards Checklist

Date: _____

Project Name: _____ Space: _____

PUBLICATIONS REQUIRED	YEAR OF EDITION	YEAR OF AMENDMENT (if required)	RESEARCH DATE
Codes and Regulations			
BUILDING CODE—Circle one: IBC NFPA 5000 OTHER _____	_____	_____	__/__/__
Structural Engineer Required? _____ YES _____ NO			
PERFORMANCE CODE—Circle one: ICCPC NFPA[1] OTHER _____	_____	_____	__/__/__
FIRE CODE—Circle one: IFC UFC OTHER _____	_____	_____	__/__/__
LIFE SAFETY CODE (NFPA 101)	_____	_____	__/__/__
PLUMBING CODE—Circle one: IPC UPC OTHER _____	_____	_____	__/__/__
Plumbing Engineer Required? _____ YES _____ NO			
MECHANICAL CODE—Circle one: IMC UMC OTHER _____	_____	_____	__/__/__
Mechanical Engineer Required? _____ YES _____ NO			
ELECTRICAL CODE—Circle one: ICCEC NEC OTHER _____	_____	_____	__/__/__
Electrical Engineer Required? _____ YES _____ NO			
ENERGY CODE/STANDARD—			
Circle one: IECC NFPA 900 OTHER _____	_____	_____	__/__/__
EPAct: ASHRAE 90.1 OTHER _____	_____	_____	__/__/__
RESIDENTIAL CODE—Circle one: IRC OTHER _____	_____	_____	__/__/__
EXISTING BUILDING CODE—Circle one: IEBC OTHER _____	_____	_____	__/__/__
SUSTAINABILITY CODE/STANDARD—Circle one: IGCC ICC 700 OTHER _____	_____	_____	__/__/__
ACCESSIBILITY REGULATIONS/STANDARDS _____			
ADA Guidelines[2]	_____	_____	__/__/__
ICC A117.1 Accessible and Usable Buildings and Facilities	_____	_____	__/__/__
Other: _____	_____	_____	__/__/__
OTHER:[3] _____	_____	_____	__/__/__
_____	_____	_____	__/__/__
Standards[4]			
NATIONAL FIRE PROTECTION ASSOCIATION (NFPA):			
NFPA _____	_____	_____	__/__/__
NFPA _____	_____	_____	__/__/__
INTERNATIONAL CODE COUNCIL (ICC)			
ICC _____	_____	_____	__/__/__
AMERICAN SOCIETY OF TESTING & MATERIALS (ASTM)			
ASTM _____	_____	_____	__/__/__
ASTM _____	_____	_____	__/__/__
UNDERWRITERS LABORATORIES (UL)			
UL _____	_____	_____	__/__/__
OTHER: _____	_____	_____	__/__/__
_____	_____	_____	__/__/__

NOTES:
1. Circle NFPA if you are using another NFPA document and plan to use a performance-based requirement listed in that document.
2. Determine if the project should follow the DA or ABA requirements.
3. Be sure to check for other state and local codes. Local codes can include special ordinances, health codes, zoning regulations, and historic preservation laws. List the specific ones.
4. Refer to the codes as well as local requirements to determine which standards are required. List the specific publications.

APPENDIX B.1 Figure 1.5 Interior Codes and Standards Checklist

Occupancy Checklist

Date: _____

Project Name: _____

Space: _____

Code Source Used (check all that apply): ____ IBC ____ LSC ____ NPFA 5000 ____ OTHER _____

Occupancy Risk Factors/Hazards (check those that apply):

__ High number of occupants
__ Occupants resting or sleeping
__ Alertness of occupants
__ Mobility of occupants
__ Age of occupants
__ Security measures

__ Occupant generally unfamiliar with space
__ Unusual characteristics of building/space
__ Potential for spread of fire
__ Hazardous materials stored or used
__ Low light levels or loud noises (typical)
__ Other: _____

Occupancy Considerations (check those that apply):[1]

__ Single Occupancy (may require more than one calculation based on types of use and/or load factors)
__ Incidental Use Areas (may need to calculate separately)
__ Accessory Occupancies (occupant load calculated separately from main occupancy; may need to include with main for exiting)
__ Separated—Mixed or Multiple Occupancy (calculate occupant load for each occupancy)
__ Non-Separated Mixed Occupancy (IBC only) (use strictest occupancy requirements)
__ Mixed Multiple Occupancy (NFPA only) (calculate occupant load for each occupancy)
__ Occupancy with Fixed Seats (may need to calculate fixed seats and surrounding open areas)
__ Accessibility Requirements (ADA guidelines, building codes, ICC A117.1 standards)

Occupant Loads[1]

Calculation 1 - Occupancy Classification: _____
Building Use (__ NEW __EXISTING): _____
__ Load Factor[2](__ GROSS __NET): _____
__ Fixed Seat Variable (__ WITH ARMS __CONTINUOUS __ BENCH): _____
Actual Floor Area (__ GROSS __NET): _____ OR Number/Length of Fixed Seats: _____
Occupant Load 1 (__ USING LOAD FACTOR FORMULA __ BASED ON FIXED SEATS): _____

Calculation 2 - Occupancy Classification: _____
Building Use (__ NEW __EXISTING): _____
__ Load Factor[2] (__ GROSS __NET): _____
__ Fixed Seat Variable (__ WITH ARMS __CONTINUOUS __ BENCH): _____
Actual Floor Area (__ GROSS __NET): _____ OR Number/Length of Fixed Seats: _____
Occupant Load 2 (__ USING LOAD FACTOR FORMULA __ BASED ON FIXED SEATS): _____

Calculation 3 - Occupancy Classification: _____
Building Use (__ NEW __EXISTING): _____
__ Load Factor[2] (__ GROSS __NET): _____
__ Fixed Seat Variable (__ WITH ARMS __CONTINUOUS __ BENCH): _____
Actual Floor Area (__ GROSS __NET): _____ OR Number/Length of Fixed Seats: _____
Occupant Load 3 (__ USING LOAD FACTOR FORMULA __ BASED ON FIXED SEATS): _____

Total Calculated Occupant Load: _____ (__ SPACE __FLOOR __ BUILDING)

Modified Occupant Load - Based on Actual Needs: _____

Local Code Approval (when required)
__ NO __YES NAME: _____ DATE: _____

NOTES:
1. If there is more than one main occupancy in the same space or building, you may want to use a separate checklist for each.
2. If you are using a gross load factor, you may need to include shared common spaces in addition to the ancillary spaces.

APPENDIX B.2 Figure 2.13 Occupancy Checklist

Means of Egress Checklist   Date: _____

Project Name: _____ Space: _____
Main Occupancy (new or existing): _____ Occupant Load: _____
Type of Space (check one): _____ Building _____ Floor _____ Space/Tenant _____ Room

---

Exit Access Requirements: (if more than 2, attach additional calculations)

Exit Access 1 (check/research those that apply and fill in the corresponding information)
Type of Component(s): __ DOOR __STAIR __ RAMP __CORRIDOR __ AISLE __ INTERVENING ROOMS
Required Width or Capacity: _____ Using: __ LEVEL VARIABLE __STAIR VARIABLE __OTHER VARIABLE
Exit Access 2 (check/research those that apply and fill in the corresponding information)
Type of Component(s): __ DOOR __STAIR __ RAMP __CORRIDOR __ AISLE __ INTERVENING ROOMS
Required Width or Capacity: _____ Using: __ LEVEL VARIABLE __STAIR VARIABLE __OTHER VARIABLE

Travel Distance (check those that apply and indicate lengths where required)
__ Common Path of Travel: _____ __ Max. allowed travel distance for space: _____
__ Dead-End Corridor: _____ __ Max. allowed travel distance for floor/building: _____

Exit Requirements: (may require up to 4 exits; if more than 2, attach additional calculations)

Required Number of Exits (check those that apply and indicate quantity where shown)
__ One Exit Exception __ Required Number of Exits: _____
__ Minimum of Two Exits __ Number of Exits Provided: _____

Location of Exits Determined by (check one)
__ 1/2 Diagonal Rule   __ Other Remoteness Requirement
__ 1/3 Diagonal Rule (if allowed)   Explain: _____

Exit 1 (Check/research those that apply and fill in the corresponding information)
Type: __ EXTERIOR DOOR __ EXIT STAIR __ EXIT PASSAGEWAY __ HORIZONTAL EXIT __ AREA OF REFUGE
Required Width: _____ Using: __ LEVEL VARIABLE __ STAIR VARIABLE __ MINIMUM REQUIRED
Number of Doors: _____ Distributed: __ EVENLY AMONG EXITS __ ASSEMBLY EXCEPTION
Exit 2 (Check/research those that apply and fill in the corresponding information)
Type: __ EXTERIOR DOOR __ EXIT STAIR __ EXIT PASSAGEWAY __ HORIZONTAL EXIT __ AREA OF REFUGE
Required Width: _____ Using: __ LEVEL VARIABLE __ STAIR VARIABLE __ MINIMUM REQUIRED
Number of Doors: _____ Distributed: __ EVENLY AMONG EXITS __ ASSEMBLY EXCEPTION

Exit Discharge Components: (Check those that apply and research if required)
__ MAIN LOBBY __ FOYER __ VESTIBULE(S) __ DISCHARGE CORRIDOR(S) __ EXIT COURT(S)

Other Code and Accessibility Requirements to Consider: (Check/research those that apply)
__ Doors: Type, Swing, Size, Hardware, Threshold, Clearances, Fire Rating
__ Stairs: Type, Riser Height, Tread Depth, Nosing, Width, Handrail, Guard, Fire Rating
__ Ramps: Slope, Rise, Landings, Width, Edge Detail, Finish, Handrail, Guard
__ Corridors: Length, Width, Protruding Objects, Fire Rating
__ Aisles: Fixed Seats, No Fixed Seats, Ramp(s), Steps, Handrails
__ Intervening Rooms: Type, Size, Obstructions, Fire Rating
__ Signage and Lighting: Exit signs, photoluminescent markings, emergency lighting, evacuation maps

---

NOTES:
1. Refer to codes and standards for specific information as well as ADA guidelines and ICC/ANSI standard for additional requirements.
2. Attach any floor plans indicating locations of components and other paperwork required for calculations.
3. Check specific occupancy classifications and/or building types for special requirements that may apply.

APPENDIX B.3 Figure 4.29 Means of Egress Checklist

Fire and Smoke Resistance Checklist Date: _____

Project Name: _____ Space: _____

Occupancy (new or existing): _____

Type of Construction: _____

REQUIRED FIRE PROTECTION (check those that apply)	EXST'G (yes/no)	LOCATION IN BUILDING	TYPE OF MATERIAL OR ASSEMBLY REQUIRED (list information)	HOURLY RATING OR FIRE TEST REQUIRED (list type)
Fire Barriers, Horizontal Assemblies, and Fire Partitions[1]				
__ Fire Wall(s)				
__ Fire Area(s)				
__ Occupancy Separation(s)				
__ Dwelling or Sleeping Unit(s)				
__ Incidental Use Areas				
__ Vertical Shaft Enclosure(s)				
__ Means of Egress Component(s)				
__ Exit Stairway(s)				
__ Exit Access Stairway(s)				
__ Horizontal Exit(s)				
__ Area(s) of Refuge				
__ Exit Corridor/ Passageway(s)				
__ Exit Access Corridor(s)				
__ Floor/Ceiling Assembly(ies)				
__ Other: _____				
Smoke Barriers and Partitions[1]				
__ Smoke Compartment(s)				
__ Vertical Shaft(s)				
__ Vestibule(s)				
__ Other: _____				
Opening Protectives				
__ Rated Door Assembly(ies)				
__ Fire Door(s)				
__ Smoke Door(s)				
__ Fire Window Assembly(ies)				
__ Rated Glazing and Frame(s)				
__ Special Hardware				
__ Other: _____				
Through-Penetration Protectives				
__ Firestop(s)				
__ Fireblocks(s)				
__ Draftstop(s)				
__ Damper System(s)				
__ Fire Damper(s)				
__ Smoke Damper(s)				
__ Other: _____				

NOTES:
1. Remember that fire and smoke assemblies must be considered both vertically and horizontally.
2. Refer to codes and standards for specific information, including sustainability codes and standards when required.
3. Check also the ADA guidelines and ICC A117.1 standard for accessibility-related requirements.
4. Attach all testing verification, including copies of manufacturer labels and/or copies of rated assembly details.

APPENDIX B.4 Figure 5.19 Fire and Smoke Resistance Checklist

Fire Protection Checklist   Date: _____

Project Name: _____ Space: _____

Main Occupancy (new or existing): _____

Type of Construction: _____

REQUIRED FIRE PROTECTION (check those that apply)	EXST'G (yes/no)	LOCATION(S) IN BUILDING	TYPE OF SYSTEM/ ITEM REQUIRED (list information)	QUANTITIES REQUIRED (new or add'l)
Detection Systems Engineer Required? ____ YES ____ NO __ Smoke Detectors(s) __ Heat Detector(s) __ Manual Fire Alarm(s) __ Other: _____				

Alarm Systems
Engineer Required? ____YES ____NO
__ Visual/Audible Alarm(s)
  __ Audible only
  __ Visual only
__ Emergency Voice/Alarm Communication System(s) (EVACS)
__ Accessible Warning System(s)
__ Other: _____				

Extinguishing Systems
Engineer Required? ____YES ____ NO
__ Fire Extinguisher(s)
__ Fire Extinguisher Cabinet(s)
__ Standpipe(s)
__ Fire Hose(s)
__ Sprinkler System(s)
  __ Types of Head(s)
  __ Orientation of Head(s)
__ Alternative Extinguishing System(s)
__Other: _____				

NOTES:

1. Refer to codes and standards for specific information as well as ADA guidelines and ICC/ANSI standard for additional requirements.

2. If an automatic sprinkler system is used, make sure it is approved and check for possible code trade-offs.

3. Consult and coordinate detection/alarm systems with electrical engineers and extinguishing systems with mechanical engineers.

4. Note on floor plans the location of fire-rated walls and floor/ceilings for placement of required fire dampers and firestops.

APPENDIX B.5 Figure 6.7 Fire Protection Checklist

Plumbing and Mechanical Checklist   **Date:** _____

Project Name: _____ Space: _____

Occupancy (new or existing): _____ Occupant Load: _____

Building Type: _____

Plumbing Requirements[2]   Engineer Required? ___ YES ___ NO

Type and Quantity of Plumbing Fixtures (check those that apply and insert quantities)

	TOTAL FIXTURES	ACCESSIBLE FIXTURES		STANDARD FIXTURES	
Fixture	**Required**	**New**	**Existing**	**New**	**Existing**
__ Water Closet	M ___/F ___	M ___/F ___	M ___/F ___	M ___/F ___	M ___/F ___
__ Urinal	M ___/F ___	M ___/F ___	M ___/F ___	M ___/F ___	M ___/F ___
__ Lavatory	M ___/F ___	M ___/F ___	M ___/F ___	M ___/F ___	M ___/F ___
__ Sink	M ___/F ___	M ___/F ___	M ___/F ___	M ___/F ___	M ___/F ___
__ Drinking Fountain	M ___/F ___	M ___/F ___	M ___/F ___	M ___/F ___	M ___/F ___
__ Bathtub	M ___/F ___	M ___/F ___	M ___/F ___	M ___/F ___	M ___/F ___
__ Shower	M ___/F ___	M ___/F ___	M ___/F ___	M ___/F ___	M ___/F ___
__ Other _____	M ___/F ___	M ___/F ___	M ___/F ___	M ___/F ___	M ___/F ___

Type of Facility Required (check those that apply)

Toilet Facilities: ____ Single (Separate M/F) ____ Single (Shared Unisex) ____ Single (Family/Assisted-Use)
                                 ____ Multi-Toilet: quantity (if more than one each M/F) _____

Bathing Facilities: ____ Single (Separate M/F) ____ Single (Shared Unisex) ____ Single (Family/Assisted-Use)
                                 ____ Multi-Bath: quantity (if more than one each M/F) _____

Other Plumbing Code/Sustainability/Accessibility Requirements (check/research those that apply)

____ Fixtures: Mounting Heights, Clear Floor Space, Faucet/Control Location, Projections, Water Consumption

____ Faucet/Controls: Ease of Operation (i.e., lever, automatic, etc.), Water Consumption, Water Temperature

____ Grab Bars: Location, Lengths, Heights, Orientation, Additional for Special Situation

____ Accessories: Mounting Heights, Control Locations, Projections, Clear Floor Space

____ Finishes: Smooth/Nonabsorbent, Slip Resistant, Thresholds, Special Locations

____ Room: Turning Space, Overlapping Clear Floor Space, Privacy, Signage, Stall Size, Door Swing

---

Mechanical Requirements[2] Engineer Required? ____ YES ____ NO

Type(s) of Mechanical System(s): _____

Mechanical Room (Size and Location): _____

Air Circulation (Type—Duct, Plenum): _____

Ventilation Required (Type and Locations): _____

Exhaust System Required (Type and Locations): _____

Ceiling Heights Required (Minimums and Clearances): _____

Supply Diffusers Required (Type and Locations—Ceiling, Wall, Floor): _____

Return Grills Required (Type and Locations—Ceiling, Wall, Floor): _____

Thermostats/Zones (Type and Locations): _____

NOTES:

1. Refer to codes and standards for specific information, including energy and sustainability codes and standards when required.

2. Check also the building codes, ICC/ANSI standard, and ADA guidelines for accessible mounting locations.

2. See Chapter 6 checklist for additional plumbing- and mechanical-related requirements such as automatic sprinkler systems, dampers, etc.

3. Be sure to note on floor plans the location of fire-rated walls/ceilings for placement of required fire/smoke stops and dampers.

APPENDIX B.6 Figure 7.14 Plumbing and Mechanical Checklist

Electrical and Communication Checklist   Date: _____

Project Name: _____ **Space:** _____

Occupancy (new or existing): _____

Electrical Requirements: Engineer Required? ___ YES ___ NO

  Types of Electrical Panels (check those that apply and note locations, sizes, etc.)

  __ Switchboard: _____

  __ Panelboard(s): _____

  __ Branch Panelboard(s): _____

Special Cabling Conditions: _____ Conduit Required: __YES __ NO

Location of Receptacle Outlets: _____

  __ EXISTING __ NEW (Rating of wall(s):_____)

Location of Switches: _____

  __ EXISTING __ NEW (Rating of wall(s): _____)

Special Types of Outlets and/or Circuits (check those that apply and note locations)

  __ Dedicated Outlets: _____

  __ Ground Fault Circuit Interrupters (GFCI): _____

  __ Arc Fault Circuit Interrupters (AFCI): _____

  __ Tamper-Resistant Outlets (dwellings): _____

  __ Other: _____

Types of Required Equipment (check those that apply, list new and existing, specify if over 120V)

  __ Light Fixtures: _____

  __ Appliances: _____

  __ Equipment: _____

Types of Electrical Systems (check those that apply, list new and existing, etc.)

  __ Emergency Electrical System: _____

  __ Required Standby System: _____

  __ Optional Standby System: _____

  __ Uninterrupted Power Supply System (UPS): _____

  __ Technical Power System (A/V): _____

Communication Requirements: Engineer Required? ___ YES ___ NO

  Type of Communication Systems3   (check those that apply and insert information)

TYPE OF CABLING SYSTEM	VENDOR OR CONSULTANT	CENTRAL LOCATION OF SYSTEM	SPECIAL NOTES
___ Telephone System			
___ Information Technology System			
___ Cable TV Services			
___ Closed-Circuit TV System			
___ Satellite TV System			
___ Voice Notification System			
___ Intercom System			
___ Assistive Listening System			
___ Audio/Visual System			
___ Security System			
___ Other			

NOTES:

1. Refer to codes and standards for specifics, including energy and sustainability codes and standards as required.

2. Check also the ADA guidelines and ICC A117.1 standard for accessible mounting locations.

2. Note on floor plans the location of fire-rated walls for placement of required fire dampers and firestops (see Chapter 5).

3. See also Chapter 6 for information on various alarm and other notification type systems as required by the codes.

APPENDIX B.7 Figure 8.10 Electrical and Communication Checklist

Date: _____

Project Name: _____

Space: _____

Occupancy (new or existing): _____

Type of Space (check one): _____ Exit _____ Exit Access _____ Other Space

REGULATED FINISHES AND FURNISHINGS (CHECK THOSE THAT APPLY)	TEST METHOD REQUIRED (FILL IN TEST NAME)	MANUFACTURER AND CATALOG #	MANUFACTURER TESTED (YES OR NO)	FINISH TREATMENT (YES OR NO)	DATE COMPLETED
Wallcoverings __ Vinyl Wallcovering __ Textile Wallcovering __ Expanded Vinyl Wallcovering __ Carpet Wallcovering __ Stretch Fabric System __ Light-Transmitting Plastics __ Wood Paneling/Veneers __ Decorative Molding/Trim __ Other: _____					
Wall Base Type: _____					
Ceiling Finishes __ Suspended Ceiling Grid __ Textile Ceiling Finish __ Stretch Fabric System __ Plastic Light-Diffusing Panels __ Decorative Ceiling __ Decorative Molding/Trim __ Other: _____					
Floor Coverings __ Carpet (Broadloom) __ Carpet Tile __ Rugs __ Carpet Padding __ Resilient Flooring __ Hardwood Flooring __ Other: _____					
Window Treatments __ Draperies __ Liners __ Blinds __ Wood Shutters __ Other: _____					
Furnishings/Furniture __ Fabric __ Vinyl/Leather __ Batting/Filling __ Welt Cord __ Interliners __ Upholstered Seating __ Mattresses __ Plastic Laminates/ Veneers __ Other: _____					

NOTES:

1. Refer to codes and standards for specific information, including the sustainability codes and standards when required.
2. Check also the ADA guidelines and ICC standard for accessibility-related finish and furniture requirements.
3. Attach all testing verifications, including copies of manufacturer labels and treatment certificates.

APPENDIX B.8 Figure 9.19 Finishes and Furniture Checklist

Summary Interior Project Checklist

Date: _____

Project Name: _____ Space: _____

1 DETERMINE WHICH CODES ARE REQUIRED (Chapter 1)

__Building Code
__Energy Code
__Fire Code
__Life Safety Code
__Performance Code
__Sustainability Code/Standard
__Other Code Publications
__Local Codes and Ordinances
__Government Regulations
__Standards and Tests

2 OCCUPANCY REQUIREMENTS (Chapter 2)

__Determine Building Types(s)
__Determine Occupancy Classification(s)
__Calculate Occupant Load(s)
__Adjustments to Occupant Load(s)
__Review Specific Occupancy Requirements
__Compare Code and Accessibility Requirements

3 MINIMUM TYPES OF CONSTRUCTION (Chapter 3)

__Determine Construction Type
__Determine Ratings of Building Elements
__Calculate Maximum Floor Area (as required)
__Calculate Building Height (as required)
__Review Construction Type Limitations

4 MEANS OF EGRESS REQUIREMENTS (Chapter 4)

__Determine Quantity and Types of Means of Egress
__Calculate Minimum Widths
__Determine Arrangement of Exits
__Calculate Travel Distance
__Determine Required Signage
__Compare Code and Accessibility Requirements
__Review Emergency Lighting Requirements

5 FIRE AND SMOKE RESISTANCE REQUIREMENTS (Chapter 5)

__Determine Use of Fire Walls
__ Determine Fire Barriers/Partitions and Horizontal Assemblies
__Determine Smoke Barriers and Partitions
__Determine Location of Opening Protectives
__Determine Location of Through-Penetration Protectives
__Review Types of Fire Tests and Ratings Required
__Determine Sustainability Requirements
__Review Requirements During Assembly Specification
__Review Required Standards

6 FIRE-PROTECTION REQUIREMENTS (Chapter 6)

__Determine Fire and Smoke Detection Systems
__Determine Required Alarm Systems
__Determine Types of Extinguishing Systems and Possible Sprinkler Trade-offs
__Compare Code and Accessibility Requirements
__Coordinate with Engineer (as required)

7 PLUMBING REQUIREMENTS (Chapter 7)

__Determine Types of Fixtures Required
__Calculate Number of Each Fixture Required
__Determine Required Toilet/Bathing Facilities
__Review for Finishes, Accessories, and Signage
__Compare Code and Accessibility Requirements
__Review Water Conservation Requirements
__Coordinate with Engineer (as required)

8 MECHANICAL REQUIREMENTS (Chapter 7)

__Determine Type of Air Distribution System(s)
__Determine Items Affecting Cooling Loads
__Determine Access and Clearance Requirements
__Figure Zoning and Thermostat Locations
__Compare Code and Accessibility Requirements
__Review Energy and Water Efficiency Compliance
__Coordinate with Engineer (as required)

9 ELECTRICAL REQUIREMENTS (Chapter 8)

__Determine Types/Locations of Outlets, Switches, Fixtures
__Determine Emergency Power and Lighting Requirements
__Compare Code and Accessibility Requirements
__Review Energy Efficiency Compliance
__Coordinate with Engineer (as required)

10 COMMUNICATION REQUIREMENTS (Chapter 8)

__Determine Systems Required by Client
__Compare Needs versus Code/Standard Requirements
__Check for Accessibility Compliance and Sustainability Requirements
__Coordinate with Engineer/Consultant (as required)

11 FINISH AND FURNITURE REQUIREMENTS (Chapter 9)

__Review Tests and Types of Ratings Required
__Determine Special Finish Requirements
__Determine Special Furniture Requirements
__Compare Code and Accessibility Requirements
__Review Sustainability Requirements
__Compare Requirements During Selection/Specification
__ Review Required Standards

NOTE: Review all codes and standards required by the local jurisdiction as well as any federal regulations that are applicable. Consult the local code offical at any step in question.

APPENDIX B.9 Figure 10.3 Summary Interior Project Checklist